NAVIGATING TURBULENCE

Navigating Turbulence

CONFLICT RESOLUTION INITIATIVES IN THE GULF AND BEYOND

GEW Reports & Analyses Team

Hichem Karoui (Editor)

Global East-West (London)

Contents

Introduction

In a rapidly changing world, conflict resolution has become a critical area of study and practice.

Nowhere is this more evident than in the Gulf region, where geopolitical tensions, domestic disputes, and transregional conflicts have posed significant challenges to stability and peace. As a researcher and editor of this collection of volumes about the Gulf, I have delved into the complex dynamics of conflict resolution in the Gulf to shed light on the strategies, approaches, and initiatives employed to address these issues.

The Arab Spring began in 2010 and profoundly impacted the Arabian Peninsula and the Gulf region. As popular uprisings, protests, and revolutions spread, the Gulf countries grappled with the far-reaching consequences of these events. The political, social, and economic ramifications of the Arab Spring have prompted a reevaluation of traditional conflict resolution techniques and the exploration of new avenues for stability.

This book is a comprehensive exploration of conflict resolution in the Gulf, examining both internal disputes within Gulf countries and the external mediation efforts undertaken by regional and international powers. It delves into the historical context of the Arab Spring's influence on the region. It analyses the lessons learned from previous conflict resolution initiatives.

One of the key aspects this book explores is the role of religious and sectarian dynamics in Gulf conflicts and their implications for conflict resolution. The Gulf region is characterized by a diversity of religious and sectarian identities, with Sunni and Shia communities often at odds. Understanding the complexities of these divisions is crucial for effective conflict resolution. The book delves into the historical roots of these divisions. It explores how various actors have manipulated or exacerbated them for political gain.

The Sunni-Shia divide in the Gulf can be traced back to the early days of Islam and the debate over succession following the death of the Prophet Muhammad. This divide has evolved over the centuries, driven by political power struggles, regional rivalries, and identity politics. In recent decades, it has been exploited by various actors in the region, fueling conflict and exacerbating tensions. Efforts to address these religious and sectarian dynamics in conflict resolution must be informed by a nuanced understanding of the historical, cultural, and socio-political factors that have shaped them.

Through in-depth case studies and analysis, this book also explores reconciliation processes in countries like Iraq and Yemen, which have faced significant internal conflicts and have become theatres for regional rivalry. By examining the different approaches in these countries, readers gain insights into the challenges and successes of various reconciliation initiatives. This book explores the strategies to rebuild fractured societies and promote sustainable peace, from power-sharing agreements to post-conflict reconstruction efforts.

In Iraq, for instance, the fall of the Saddam Hussein regime in 2003 unleashed a wave of violence and internal power struggles. The sectarian tensions between the Sunni minority and the Shia majority escalated, leading to a protracted and devastating conflict. The book explores how international actors and Iraqi leaders have attempted to reconcile these divisions through initiatives such as the National Reconciliation Program and the convening of national dialogues. By analyzing the successes and failures of these initiatives, readers gain a deeper understanding of the challenges and complexities of conflict resolution in a deeply divided society.

Similarly, Yemen has been embroiled in a multifaceted conflict since 2014, pitting various factions against one another.

The Houthi rebel group, backed by Iran, has fought against the internationally recognized government, which has received support from a Saudi-led coalition.

This intricate web of alliances and rivalries has posed significant challenges to conflict resolution efforts. The book examines the efforts of international mediators, such as the United Nations, to broker a political settlement and mitigate the humanitarian crisis. It also highlights the role of local actors and traditional dispute-resolution mechanisms in achieving sustainable peace.

In addition, this book evaluates the role of Oman as a mediator in the reconciliation of the Gulf countries.

Oman has long been recognized for its diplomatic efforts. It has played a crucial role in facilitating dialogue and understanding between rival factions. By analyzing Oman's mediation approach, readers gain valuable insights into the methods and principles that have made it a successful mediator in such complex and challenging situations. For example, Oman's efforts in mediating the Iran-Saudi Arabia tensions have contributed to de-escalating regional rivalries and creating a conducive environment for conflict resolution.

Transregional issues such as illegal migration, drug trafficking, and terrorism are also examined in the context of conflict resolution efforts in the Gulf. These issues not only exacerbate existing conflicts but also have broader regional implications. By understanding the interconnectedness of these challenges, readers can better grasp the complex web of dynamics at play and develop more comprehensive conflict resolution strategies.

The book explores the role of regional cooperation frameworks, such as the Gulf Cooperation Council (GCC), in addressing these transregional challenges and promoting peace and stability.

Furthermore, this book delves into conflict resolution initiatives in broader regional conflicts, particularly in Sudan, Libya, and Syria, and the impact of the Ukraine war on Gulf conflict resolution efforts. Recognizing the spill-over effects of regional conflicts on the Gulf and vice versa, the book explores the strategies employed to address these broader regional challenges and their impact on stability and peace in the Gulf.

In Sudan, for example, the mediation efforts led by the African Union and backed by the Gulf countries played a crucial role in brokering a power-sharing agreement between the military and civilian representatives after President Omar al-Bashir was overthrown. The book examines the challenges faced during this mediation process and the steps taken to ensure sustainable peace.

In conclusion, this book presents a deeper understanding of the challenges and possibilities for conflict resolution in the Gulf region. By critically examining the factors and dynamics that have shaped conflicts in the Gulf, readers will gain valuable insights that can inform future efforts to resolve existing disputes and prevent new ones from emerging. Through in-depth case studies, historical analysis, and an exploration of regional and transregional dynamics, this book provides a comprehensive framework for understanding and addressing conflicts in the Gulf. It is an essential resource for scholars, policymakers, and practitioners seeking to contribute to peacebuilding efforts in the region.

Hichem Karoui (Research Director and Editor).

1

Historical Context

THE IMPACT OF THE ARAB SPRING IN THE GULF

The Arab Spring, a wave of protests and uprisings that swept across the Middle East and North Africa, had a profound and lasting impact on the Gulf region.

While the Gulf countries were relatively stable compared to other Arab states, they, too, experienced significant repercussions from the movements for democracy and political reform. This chapter aims to delve deeper into the historical context surrounding the Arab Spring in the Gulf, analysing its causes, manifestations, and consequences within the region, with a comprehensive exploration of each Gulf country.

Root Causes of the Arab Spring in the Gulf

The underlying causes of the Arab Spring in the Gulf varied across the region. Political repression, social inequality, economic grievances, and demands for greater political participation were the key factors driving the uprisings. In Saudi Arabia, for instance, high youth unemployment, limited political freedoms, and widespread corruption fuelled discontent among the population. The ruling House of Saud, known for its tight control over political power, faced mounting challenges as a significant portion of the people, particularly the younger generation, sought political reform and an end to royal autocracy.

Similarly, Kuwait faced issues of political marginalisation and corruption, leading to calls for political reform. The Kuwaiti government, dominated by an elite ruling family, struggled to address widespread discontent among the population. Demands for greater transparency, accountability, and inclusivity resonated with Kuwait's diverse society, which is comprised not only of ethnic Kuwaitis but also of a sizable expatriate population.

In the UAE, economic disparities, restrictive laws, and limited political representation triggered demands for change. Despite rapid modernisation and economic growth, a significant portion of the population faced challenges such as joblessness, low wages, and limited social mobility. Calls for more equitable distribution of wealth and political power emerged from various segments of society, including Emiratis and expatriates, who played a critical role in the Gulf nation's economy.

Protests and Uprisings in the Gulf

While the Gulf region experienced the impact of the Arab Spring, certain countries witnessed more pronounced protests and uprisings. Bahrain and Oman, in particular, faced significant challenges during this period. In Bahrain, a majority Shi'a population demanded political reforms and an end to discrimination perpetuated by the ruling Sunni minority. What began as peaceful protests in February 2011 quickly escalated into violence as the government responded with a heavy-handed crackdown. The Bahraini government, with backing from Saudi Arabia, declared a state of emergency, leading to prolonged unrest, strained sectarian tensions, and allegations of human rights abuses.

Oman, led by Sultan Qaboos bin Said al Said, witnessed protests demanding better living conditions, employment opportunities, and an end to corruption. Recognising the protesters' legitimate demands, Sultan Qaboos initiated a series of reforms and introduced new policies to address their grievances. He reshuffled his cabinet, increased welfare spending, and promised job creation. These measures, combined with engaging in dialogue with the protesters, helped alleviate tensions and restore relative stability in Oman.

Repression and Countermeasures

Fearful of the spread of unrest, the Gulf governments employed different strategies to quell the uprisings. Some countries, like Bahrain and Saudi Arabia, resorted to harsh repression, employing security forces and cracking down on dissent. Bahrain, in particular, faced widespread condemnation for its excessive use of force against protesters, including arbitrary arrests, torture, and forced disappearances. The Bahraini government enacted emergency laws and imposed strict media censorship to suppress information about the protests and control the narrative about the unrest.

Saudi Arabia took a firm stance against any dissent that might challenge the long-standing monarchy. The government deployed its security forces to quash protests and employed heavy-handed tactics to crush any opposition. Additionally, it enacted more restrictive legislation, further limiting freedom of speech and tightening control over civil society activities.

On the other hand, countries such as Oman and Qatar took a more conciliatory approach. As mentioned earlier, Oman initiated reforms and engaged in dialogue with protesters to alleviate their concerns. Sultan Qaboos, widely regarded as a reform-minded leader, recognised the importance of addressing the demands of the population for political and socioeconomic change. In Qatar, while relatively spared from significant domestic unrest, the government responded to the regional context of the Arab Spring by increasing welfare spending, enacting labour reforms, and allowing for greater freedom of expression. These measures aimed to address underlying grievances and reduce the potential for dissatisfaction in protests.

External Factors and Geostrategic Implications

The impact of the Arab Spring in the Gulf was not limited to internal dynamics alone; external factors and regional alliances played crucial roles. The Gulf Cooperation Council (GCC) countries, led by Saudi Arabia, were concerned about the potential spillover effects of the uprisings, particularly from Bahrain and Yemen. They viewed these popular movements as part of a broader regional contestation for power and influence. As a result, Saudi Arabia provided significant financial, diplomatic, and even military support to bolster neighbouring regimes and suppress dissent.

The broader regional rivalry between Saudi Arabia and Iran also exacerbated tensions. It influenced the response to the Arab Spring within the Gulf.

Saudi Arabia, predominantly Sunni, and Iran, a Shia-majority country, have long competed for regional dominance.

The fear of Iranian influence and potential Shia uprisings fuelled a sense of urgency among the Gulf monarchies to maintain their grip on power and prevent significant reforms that might empower more marginalised communities.

Consequences and Lessons Learnt

The consequences of the Arab Spring in the Gulf were substantial and far-reaching. While some governments implemented limited reforms to appease their populations, they also reinforced control mechanisms and tightened surveillance on dissent. The protests forced Gulf countries to acknowledge and address long-standing grievances, including state corruption, unemployment, and economic disparities.

However, despite the initial demands for reform, the governments in the Gulf were mainly able to contain the uprisings. They fortified their regimes by adopting security measures, economic concessions, and limited political reforms to maintain the status quo. Nevertheless, the protests left an indelible mark on the societal consciousness. They challenged the perception of the Gulf states as immune to popular demands for change.

Moreover, the uprisings highlighted the importance of engaging with the youth population, promoting inclusive governance, and addressing socioeconomic challenges to prevent future social unrest. The governments in the Gulf recognised the need to diversify their economies, enhance job creation, and improve the overall quality of life for their citizens. This acknowledgement led to a renewed focus on economic development, innovation, and fostering social cohesion.

To Sum Up

In conclusion, the Arab Spring profoundly impacted the Gulf region, leading to protests, reforms, and state responses that continue to shape the political and social landscape. This chapter provided an in-depth analysis of the historical context surrounding the Arab Spring in each Gulf country, highlighting the diverse causes, manifestations, and consequences witnessed across the region.

Understanding this nuanced historical context is crucial to comprehending subsequent chapters on conflict resolution initiatives in the Gulf and the broader Middle East. By delving deeper into the specifics of each Gulf nation's experience during the Arab Spring, we can enhance our understanding of the complexities and challenges faced by each country and the lessons learnt from this transformative period in Gulf history. These lessons will lay the foundation for a more comprehensive analysis of the conflict resolution efforts and their effectiveness in subsequent chapters.

2

Conflict Resolution Techniques

LESSONS FROM PAST INITIATIVES

Conflict is an inevitable part of human interaction. Throughout history, societies and civilisations have sought ways to resolve disputes peacefully.

This chapter examines conflict resolution techniques through historical examples.

By analysing these past efforts, we can glean valuable insights and apply them to current conflicts in the Gulf and beyond.

Identifying the Underlying Causes

The first step in effective conflict resolution is understanding the root causes behind the dispute. Identifying the underlying political, economic, social, or cultural issues. Past initiatives have demonstrated the need for comprehensive analysis, as addressing surface-level disagreements without addressing the deeper causes often leads to unresolved tensions and recurring conflicts.

To gain a deeper understanding of the underlying causes, stakeholders should undertake a thorough assessment that includes a historical review, stakeholder analysis, and identification of key drivers. We can identify recurring patterns and systemic issues contributing to conflicts by examining historical precedents. For example, in the Gulf region, conflicts may stem from power struggles between regional powers, competition for resources, or deep-seated religious and cultural differences.

Stakeholder analysis involves identifying and understanding the individuals or groups directly or indirectly impacted by the conflict, their interests, and their relative importance.

Moreover, recognising the critical drivers behind conflicts, such as power dynamics, resource scarcity, inequality, or identity-based issues, allows for a nuanced understanding of the root causes and aids in formulating targeted solutions.

COMMUNICATION AND DIALOGUE

Open and constructive communication is fundamental in any conflict resolution process. Past initiatives have emphasised the importance of creating an environment that encourages all parties to express their concerns, interests, and grievances. Dialogue facilitates understanding, helps build trust, and creates opportunities for discovering common ground. Lessons from previous initiatives underscore the significance of active listening, empathy, and respecting diverse perspectives.

In addition to fostering communication, it is essential to establish structured platforms and processes for dialogue. These platforms can range from formal negotiations to informal discussions, community forums, or even culturally specific traditions for dispute resolution. Including unbiased facilitators trained in conflict resolution techniques and skilled in managing power dynamics can help ensure a balanced conversation. Creating a safe space where participants can freely express their views and concerns without fear of retribution encourages open dialogue and cooperation.

Mediation and Facilitation

The involvement of neutral mediators or facilitators can significantly contribute to successful conflict resolution. Third-party intervention provides a balanced perspective and ensures that all parties receive fair treatment. Past initiatives have highlighted the importance of selecting mediators with cultural sensitivity, impartiality, and exceptional negotiation skills. Mediators help bridge gaps, foster compromise, and guide discussions toward mutually agreeable solutions.

Effective mediators facilitate open communication channels, ensuring parties have equal opportunities to present their views. They help clarify misunderstandings, reframe issues, and promote empathy among participants. The mediator's role extends beyond simply facilitating dialogue; they should also assist in structuring the negotiation process, managing power imbalances, and creating an environment conducive to creativity and compromise. Mediation may require multiple sessions, where mediators employ various techniques, such as shuttle diplomacy (where mediators move between parties separately), joint problem-solving (where parties collaborate to find standard solutions), or caucusing (where mediators meet privately with each party), depending on the context and needs of the parties involved.

Negotiation and Compromise

Achieving a lasting resolution often requires negotiation and compromise. Past initiatives have showcased the significance of finding common interests and seeking win-win outcomes. Negotiation techniques, such as interest-based bargaining and problem-solving approaches, have proven effective in managing conflicts. Creating an atmosphere conducive to compromise and offering incentives can facilitate reaching mutually acceptable agreements.

Successful negotiation relies on an integrative approach to expand the pie and create value for all parties involved. By exploring underlying interests rather than fixed positions, negotiators can find innovative solutions that address the concerns of everyone involved. However, compromise does not imply sacrificing core values or principles; it requires creative problem-solving, exploring alternatives, and prioritising long-term stability and cooperation over short-term gains. To achieve sustainable outcomes, negotiators should ensure that agreements are based on shared values, mutual respect, and a commitment to upholding the interests and rights of all parties.

Building Trust and Confidence

Rebuilding trust is crucial in conflict resolution. Past initiatives have emphasised the need to establish confidence-building measures demonstrating a genuine commitment to resolving the conflict. Transparency, accountability, and consistent agreement adherence are essential for fostering trust among conflicting parties. Lessons from past initiatives underscore the significance of incremental steps and small victories in building trust and confidence over time.

Trust-building requires ongoing efforts from all stakeholders involved in the conflict resolution process. Transparent communication, confidentiality when necessary, and honouring commitments are vital to building trust. Additionally, confidence-building measures can include joint projects, cultural exchanges, or other activities that foster interaction and foster understanding among conflicting parties. To ensure sustainability, it is crucial to establish mechanisms to monitor and verify compliance with agreed-upon commitments, reinforcing the trust-building process.

Inclusive and Participatory Approaches

Successful conflict resolution initiatives promote inclusivity and encourage the participation of all stakeholders. Engaging diverse perspectives and ensuring that marginalised voices are heard is crucial for sustainable solutions. Past initiatives have taught us the importance of involving critical actors in decision-making, as their ownership and commitment are vital for the success of any resolution effort.

Inclusivity fosters a sense of ownership, legitimacy, and effectiveness in resolving conflicts. Genuine efforts to include marginalised groups, women, youth, and other underrepresented voices provide a holistic perspective and enhance the legitimacy of the resulting solutions. Involving all stakeholders in designing, implementing, and monitoring conflict resolution interventions ensures a comprehensive understanding of the root causes. It increases the likelihood of successful and sustainable outcomes. Moreover, inclusive approaches help build social cohesion, minimise future grievances, and strengthen relationships among diverse communities.

Learning from Failures and Adaptability

Conflict resolution is sometimes linear or straightforward, and failures are inevitable. Learning from past failures allows for adapting strategies, approaches, and techniques. Examining previous initiatives helps identify pitfalls to avoid. It enables the incorporation of lessons learnt into future attempts at conflict resolution.

Evaluating and reflecting on past initiatives is crucial for iterative learning and improvement. Careful examination of failed initiatives helps identify areas of weakness, potential biases, or inadequate approaches that may have hindered progress. Stakeholders can adapt their strategies, policies, and interventions by critically analysing setbacks. Flexibility and adaptability are critical attributes for conflict resolution practitioners, as they must navigate complex and evolving dynamics while remaining open to innovative approaches and embracing continuous learning.

To Sum Up

The techniques and lessons from past conflict resolution initiatives provide valuable insights for addressing the challenges in the Gulf and beyond. We can pave the way towards lasting resolutions by understanding the complexities of conflicts, fostering dialogue, involving neutral mediators, promoting compromise, building trust, and embracing inclusivity. Through these lessons, we begin to shape a future where peaceful co-existence can thrive.

3

Conflict Resolution

WITHIN GULF/ARABIAN
PENINSULA STATES

Conflict resolution within the Gulf/Arabian Peninsula states is a complex and multifaceted process that requires a thorough understanding of the region's dynamics, history, and cultural context. The Gulf countries, including Saudi Arabia, Kuwait, United Arab Emirates, Qatar, Oman, and Bahrain, have experienced various internal conflicts, ranging from political and sectarian tensions.

Dialogue and negotiation serve as fundamental approaches to conflict resolution within Gulf states. Bringing together different stakeholders, including government officials, religious leaders, tribal representatives, and civil society actors, provides a platform to discuss and address the underlying causes of conflict.

These dialogues occur at various levels, including national, regional, and local, to ensure that all perspectives are considered and represented for effective conflict resolution.

Mediation and facilitation by external actors play a crucial role in conflict resolution processes within Gulf states. Experienced mediators assist in bridging communication gaps, building trust, and fostering an environment conducive to reaching mutually acceptable solutions. The involvement of trusted external actors, such as the United Nations or regional organisations like the Arab League, can provide impartiality and expertise in facilitating negotiations, reducing the risk of biased outcomes.

The Gulf/Arabian Peninsula region has a rich history of traditional conflict resolution practices complementing formal mechanisms. Conventional methods, such as tribal mediation and reconciliation processes, have proven effective in resolving local community disputes. These conventional practices draw upon centuries-old wisdom, cultural norms, and a deep understanding of regional dynamics. Integrating these traditional approaches with formal conflict resolution mechanisms can enhance the effectiveness and cultural appropriateness of the overall process.

Inclusivity is a vital element of conflict resolution within Gulf states. These deeply divided societies with differing political, religious, and tribal affiliations require the recognition and participation of all relevant parties to ensure a sense of ownership and legitimacy in the decision-making process. In addition to formal state institutions, non-state actors, including activists, women's groups, youth organisations, and religious and tribal leaders, must be included to promote a comprehensive and inclusive approach to conflict resolution. This inclusivity promotes trust-building, reduces marginalisation, and contributes to sustainable peace.

Economic and social development initiatives are critical in conflict resolution within Gulf states. Addressing underlying socio-economic grievances, such as unemployment, poverty, and inequality, is essential to alleviate tensions and create a conducive environment for peaceful coexistence. Governments can invest in education, healthcare, infrastructure, and job creation to provide opportunities for the population, reducing the factors contributing to conflict. Equitable distribution of resources and inclusive economic policies can help address grievances and promote a sense of fairness.

Learning from successful conflict resolution initiatives in other regions is valuable for Gulf states. Studying best practices and lessons learnt can provide insights into effective mechanisms such as transitional justice, truth, and reconciliation commissions, which can contribute to healing and reconciliation. Additionally, understanding the role of civil society organisations in peacebuilding processes and their contributions to fostering social cohesion can help develop tailored approaches within the Gulf context. Collaboration and knowledge-sharing with international actors, academic institutions, and think tanks can significantly enhance regional conflict resolution efforts.

However, it is crucial to recognise that conflict resolution within the Gulf/Arabian Peninsula states is a complex and long-term endeavour. It demands sustained commitment from all stakeholders, including governments, civil society organisations, and external actors. Furthermore, regional conflicts are often interconnected with broader regional and international dynamics, necessitating a comprehensive and holistic approach to finding peaceful resolutions. Cooperation and coordination with neighbouring countries and regional organisations are essential to addressing transnational conflicts and ensuring stability and security in the wider Gulf region.

Regional organisations, such as the Gulf Cooperation Council (GCC), can play a significant role in conflict resolution. The GCC has the potential to enhance cooperation, facilitate dialogue, and support mediation efforts among its member states. It can also serve as a platform for sharing experiences, lessons learnt, and best practices in conflict resolution, contributing to a collective understanding of effective strategies. Strengthening regional mechanisms for conflict prevention, early warning systems, and peacebuilding can provide a framework for sustained peace and stability in the Gulf/Arabian Peninsula states.

Furthermore, cultural sensitivity is essential when approaching conflict resolution within Gulf states. Understanding the intricacies of local customs, traditions, and social structures is necessary to navigate complex dynamics. Engaging with local religious and tribal leaders with significant influence can help bridge divides and promote reconciliation efforts. Respect for cultural diversity and the rights of minority groups is central to building sustainable peace in the region. Investing in inter-cultural dialogue and fostering a culture of tolerance and co-existence can contribute to long-term peace and stability within Gulf states.

To sum up, conflict resolution within the Gulf/Arabian Peninsula states necessitates an inclusive dialogue, socio-economic development, external mediation, and learning from successful conflict resolution experiences. Gulf states can work towards a more stable and harmonious future by addressing the root causes of conflict, promoting inclusivity, and investing in sustainable peacebuilding strategies. The commitment of all stakeholders and the recognition of regional dynamics are crucial in fostering peace and mitigating conflicts within the Gulf/Arabian Peninsula states. Coordinated efforts within the region and with external actors are essential to achieving lasting peace in this diverse and strategically important region.

4

Internal Conflict Dynamics

EXPLORING ROOT CAUSES

Internal conflicts have plagued societies throughout history, and the Gulf region is no exception. Understanding their root causes is crucial to effectively addressing and resolving these conflicts. This chapter aims to delve into the internal conflict dynamics within Gulf states, shedding light on the underlying factors that contribute to such conflicts.

HISTORICAL CONTEXT

Examining the historical context provides valuable insights into the foundations of internal conflicts within the Gulf region.

The Gulf states have emerged from a complex history of colonisation, tribal rivalries, and power struggles. During the 19th and 20th centuries, colonial powers, namely Great Britain, France, and the Ottoman Empire, played significant roles in shaping the region's boundaries, often without considering the tribal, ethnic, and sectarian composition of the populations. These arbitrary borderlines have exacerbated tensions and deepened historical grievances, leading to territorial and identity conflicts.

SOCIOECONOMIC FACTORS

Socioeconomic factors are critical determinants of internal conflicts within Gulf states. While the region is known for its wealth and oil reserves, economic disparities exist, leading to feelings of marginalisation and social inequities. Despite the immense economic growth, vast resources have sometimes translated into broad-based benefits for the population. Policies favouring elite groups, corruption, and mismanagement of public funds have resulted in limited opportunities for social mobility and economic diversification. High youth unemployment rates, particularly among university graduates, exacerbate frustrations and societal discontent. Additionally, the reliance on oil revenues leaves Gulf states vulnerable to global economic fluctuations, which can amplify social and economic tensions.

POLITICAL SYSTEMS

The nature of political systems within Gulf states is crucial in understanding the root causes of internal conflicts. Most Gulf states are characterised by autocratic rule, limiting political participation and suppressing dissent. Power is often concentrated in the hands of ruling families, leading to a need for accountable governance structures and transparency. This lack of political openness and citizen engagement creates a breeding ground for grievances, as citizens cannot voice their concerns and hold their governments accountable. The absence of inclusive governance structures and mechanisms for citizen participation further alienates certain groups within society, increasing the potential for social unrest.

SECTARIAN AND ETHNIC DIVISIONS

Sectarian and ethnic divisions play significant roles in internal conflicts within the Gulf region. The diverse ethnic and religious composition of societies can be a source of strength. Still, it can also lead to tension and conflict, particularly when combined with economic disparities and political marginalisation. Sectarian divisions, rooted in historical and religious differences, have been exploited by regional and international actors seeking to gain influence, exacerbating conflicts within Gulf states. Furthermore, the rhetoric and actions of some political actors, both nationally and regionally, have polarised communities and deepened divisions, hindering efforts for social cohesion.

REGIONAL AND INTERNATIONAL INFLUENCE

The role of regional and international actors in exacerbating or mitigating internal conflicts within the Gulf must be considered. The Gulf states often encounter regional power struggles and proxy wars that transcend national borders. Rivalries between Iran and Saudi Arabia, for example, have spilt over into conflicts within Bahrain, Iraq, and Yemen, intensifying internal dynamics. External interventions, driven by geopolitical interests, further complicate the situation, prolonging conflicts and impeding peaceful resolutions. Moreover, the Gulf states' strategic importance in the global energy market attracts the attention of major powers, increasing their involvement in the region's internal dynamics.

RELIGIOUS EXTREMISM AND IDEOLOGICAL POLARISATION

Religious extremism and ideological polarisation are additional factors that contribute to internal conflicts within Gulf states. The rise of extremist groups, such as the Islamic State (IS) and Al-Qaeda, has not only affected neighbouring countries but also had repercussions within the Gulf. Marginalised individuals, feeling disillusioned by their socioeconomic conditions and perceived injustices, are vulnerable to the recruitment efforts of these extremist organisations. The sectarian divide in the region has also fuelled ideological polarisation, deepening existing societal fault lines and presenting a challenge to struggles for social cohesion and stability.

TO SUM UP

Understanding the root causes of conflicts within Gulf states is crucial for effective conflict resolution. By examining the historical context, socioeconomic factors, political systems, sectarian divisions, regional influences, and the impact of religious extremism and ideological polarisation, a comprehensive understanding of the internal conflict dynamics in the region can be achieved. To address these root causes, promoting inclusive governance, implementing socioeconomic reforms that reduce disparities, and fostering social cohesion is essential. Diplomatic efforts to de-escalate regional tensions and resolve conflicts in neighbouring countries can positively ripple effect on internal dynamics within Gulf states. Ultimately, sustainable peace and stability can be achieved in the Gulf region through concerted efforts to address and resolve these root causes of internal conflicts.

5

Mediation by External Powers

RESOLVING GULF COUNTRY DIFFERENCES

In the context of Gulf conflict resolution, external powers have played a significant role in mediating and resolving conflicts between Gulf countries. This chapter delves deeper into the various mediation efforts made by external powers and their impact on resolving differences among Gulf countries, considering historical context, challenges, successes, results, limitations, and prospects.

1. HISTORICAL CONTEXT

External powers' involvement in Gulf conflicts dates back to the colonial era when European powers exerted influence over the region. The British Empire, in particular, controlled territories and established protectorates, shaping the political landscape and dynamics in the Gulf. This historical backdrop deeply influences current conflicts and external mediation efforts in the region.

Additionally, the end of World War II and the subsequent decolonisation process greatly impacted the Gulf region. As colonial powers withdrew, new nation-states emerged, shifting power dynamics and creating fertile ground for conflicts. Gulf countries' newfound independence was accompanied by territorial disputes, conflicting interests, and struggles for influence, laying the foundation for external powers to intervene in mediation efforts.

2. MEDIATION INITIATIVES BY EXTERNAL POWERS

a) The United States: As a global power, the US has been actively mediating conflicts in the Gulf. Its interests include maintaining stability for economic and strategic reasons, securing energy resources, and ensuring regional security. The US utilises its diplomatic leverage, led by the State Department, and engages in various mediation mechanisms, such as shuttle diplomacy and hosting peace conferences.

Over the decades, the US has consistently committed to Gulf conflict mediation. From the Camp David Accords between

Egypt and Israel in 1978 to the recent efforts to resolve the Qatar-Gulf Cooperation Council (GCC) crisis, the US has utilised its leverage and diplomatic networks to bring disputing parties to the negotiating table.

b) The United Nations: The UN has been instrumental in facilitating dialogue and promoting peace between Gulf countries. It deploys special envoys or mediators who engage in shuttle diplomacy, hosting peace talks, and providing technical assistance. The UN's involvement legitimises the mediation process and encourages parties to participate in negotiations.

One notable example of the UN's mediation efforts in the Gulf is the Iran-Iraq war (1980-1988). The UN Security Council was crucial in ceasefire negotiations and coordinating peace-keeping efforts. Although lengthy and challenging, the mediation process eventually led to a resolution and the cessation of hostilities.

c) Regional Powers: Countries in the broader Middle East, such as Egypt, Turkey, and Pakistan, have also participated in mediation efforts. They leverage their historical relationships, cultural ties, and economic influence to facilitate dialogue and reconciliation between conflicting parties. These regional powers often play supportive roles with global authorities or intergovernmental organisations.

For example, during the GCC crisis that erupted in June 2017, Kuwait took on the role of mediator. Leveraging its neutral position, historical ties, and reputation as a regional peacemaker, Kuwait engaged in shuttle diplomacy, hosting multiple talks to resolve the crisis. While the problem is not entirely resolved, Kuwait's mediation efforts have shown progress and provide a glimmer of hope for future reconciliation.

3. CHALLENGES AND SUCCESSES

Mediating conflicts in the Gulf region poses several challenges. These include complex dynamics within Gulf countries, deep-rooted rivalries, historical grievances, diverse ideological positions, and geopolitical considerations. The presence of non-state actors, such as extremist groups and transnational organisations, further complicates peacebuilding efforts. Economic dependencies, resource competition, and power struggles also make finding common ground and lasting solutions challenging.

However, successes have been achieved through sustained engagement, diplomatic pressure, and leveraging economic, political, and military incentives to encourage conflict parties towards compromise. The 2015 Iran nuclear deal, known as the Joint Comprehensive Plan of Action (JCPOA), is a significant success in Gulf conflict mediation. Through diplomatic negotiations, the P5+1 countries (the US, UK, France, Germany, Russia, and China) agreed with Iran, easing tensions and opening the door for better relations.

4. IMPACTS AND LIMITATIONS

a) Positive impacts: The involvement of external powers in Gulf conflict resolution has led to several positive outcomes. These include de-escalating tensions, increased dialogue, and potential long-term peace and stability. External mediation catalyses initiating negotiations and provides a platform for all parties to voice their concerns, aiding in developing trust-building measures.

External powers often bring resources and expertise, supporting post-conflict reconstruction and development efforts. The influx of financial, technological, or infrastructural assistance can contribute to stability and foster positive interdependence between formerly conflicting countries.

b) Limitations: Despite the positive impacts, external mediation also faces limitations. Accusations of biased mediation, external interference in domestic affairs, and concerns over external powers' long-term commitment and influence can hinder the mediation process. Additionally, the lack of a comprehensive regional security framework, differing interests among external actors, and the unwillingness of disputing parties to compromise can slow progress.

Furthermore, achieving sustainable peace requires addressing deep-rooted societal divisions, promoting inclusive governance, and building community trust. External mediation should be mindful of these factors and work towards empowering local actors and fostering domestic ownership of the conflict resolution process.

5. FUTURE PROSPECTS

The future of external mediation in resolving Gulf country differences depends on various factors. The willingness of disputing parties to engage in dialogue, the region's geopolitical dynamics, the capacities of external mediators, and the inclusivity of the peace process all play significant roles.

Multi-track diplomacy, involving a combination of official negotiations, people-to-people dialogue, civil society engagement, and economic incentives, can enhance the prospects of successful mediation. Investing in long-term conflict prevention and reconciliation measures can also help build sustainable peace in the Gulf region.

External powers must embrace a multidimensional approach that addresses the immediate manifestations of conflict and its underlying causes. This involves addressing socio-economic disparities, promoting human rights, and fostering intra-regional cooperation. By doing so, external mediators can help create an enabling environment for dialogue, reconciliation, and sustainable peace in the Gulf.

By analysing external powers' past and ongoing mediation efforts, this chapter highlights the historical, geopolitical, and socio-cultural factors influencing resolving conflicts in the Gulf. It reveals the complexities, challenges, and opportunities external mediators face. It underscores the need for inclusive and sustainable peacebuilding processes in the region. The continued engagement of external powers, working in collaboration with regional actors, will be essential to navigate and resolve the intricate conflicts Gulf countries face.

6

Regional Implications of Gulf Conflict

The Gulf region has long been a hotbed of conflicts and tensions, with significant regional implications extending far beyond its borders. The various conflicts within the Gulf have intensified within the region, sparked concerns among neighbouring countries, and shaped the geopolitical landscape of the broader Middle East and beyond. This chapter will delve deeper into the multifaceted regional implications of Gulf conflicts, highlighting the ripple effects on neighbouring states, regional stability, the global economy, and the broader international order.

IMPACT ON NEIGHBOURING COUNTRIES

Gulf conflicts have inevitably affected neighbouring countries in profound ways, rippling through their societies and economies. The spillover effect of disputes, such as the ongoing Yemeni civil war or the past Iran-Iraq war, has resulted in a flow of refugees, increased security threats, and economic disruptions. Bordering states are forced to address these challenges, bearing the burden of hosting displaced populations, managing security risks, and navigating the financial consequences of conflict.

For instance, the Yemeni civil war, which started in 2015, has created a dire humanitarian crisis with a staggering death toll, widespread famine, and an ongoing cholera epidemic. This has directly impacted neighbouring countries such as Saudi Arabia and Oman, which have borne the brunt of the crisis. Saudi Arabia, in particular, has faced security challenges due to cross-border missile attacks launched by Houthi rebels in Yemen. Moreover, both Saudi Arabia and Oman have been grappling with an influx of Yemeni refugees, straining their resources, social fabric, and infrastructure. The conflict's spillover has also led to an increase in terrorist activities, particularly by Al-Qaeda in the Arabian Peninsula (AQAP), posing a security threat to the entire region.

Similarly, the Iran-Iraq war from 1980 to 1988 had far-reaching consequences for neighbouring states. The conflict, with its roots in territorial disputes and ideological differences, had a profound impact on Kuwait and Saudi Arabia. Both countries provided significant financial and material support to Iraq, fearing the spread of Iranian revolutionary ideals and a potential threat to their stability. In retaliation, Iran targeted Kuwaiti and Saudi installations, necessitating international protection and military intervention to safeguard vital resources and maintain regional stability. The conflict disrupted trade routes, threatened oil installations, and heightened regional tensions, leaving a lasting impact on the peace and prosperity of neighbouring nations.

REGIONAL STABILITY

The conflicts within the Gulf have far-reaching ramifications for regional stability, creating a web of interconnected challenges that perpetuate tensions and divisions. Escalating internal conflicts can ignite broader regional conflicts and exacerbate pre-existing fault lines. As conflicts intensify, regional states may be drawn into proxy wars or compelled to take sides, thus heightening divisions and contributing to further instability.

One of the critical fault lines in the Gulf region lies in the long-standing animosity between Saudi Arabia and Iran. Geopolitical competition, religious differences, and power struggles characterise the rivalry between these major players. Gulf conflicts often serve as battlegrounds for this power struggle, with proxies engaging in regional competitions. The ongoing conflicts in Syria, Yemen, and Bahrain are all deeply influenced by Saudi-Iranian tensions, drawing regional and international actors into the fray.

Furthermore, regional conflicts have triggered a rise in extremist ideologies and sectarian tensions, further fuelling instability in the wider region. Militant groups such as ISIS and its affiliates have exploited the power vacuums created by Gulf conflicts, destabilising Iraq, Syria, and beyond. The spread of these extremist ideologies poses a direct threat to regional and global security, necessitating concerted efforts to counter radicalisation and address the root causes fuelling these conflicts.

GLOBAL ECONOMY

The Gulf region plays a significant role in the global economy, primarily due to its vast oil and gas reserves. Any disruptions in the area resulting from conflicts can have profound implications for global energy markets, trade flows, and economic stability. The 1990 Gulf War, triggered by Iraq's invasion of Kuwait, had a profound impact on global oil prices and supply. Oil prices spiked, causing market volatility, while supply disruptions forced countries to find alternative sources, leading to speculative price increases and economic downturns in numerous nations. The fear of potential disruptions to oil supply from Gulf conflicts continues to have a ripple effect, influencing the dynamics of global energy security and impacting global economic stability.

Moreover, Gulf conflicts have led to an increase in terrorism and the spread of extremist ideologies, creating a global security challenge. The rise of ISIS, for example, gained momentum due to the conflicts in Syria and Iraq, attracting foreign fighters from around the world and spreading its influence to different parts of the globe. The need for international cooperation and coordination to counter the global threat posed by terrorism originating from Gulf conflicts has become crucial, necessitating alliances, intelligence sharing, and concerted efforts to dismantle terrorist networks and ideologies.

EFFORTS AT REGIONAL CONFLICT RESOLUTION

Despite the complexities and regional implications of Gulf conflicts, various initiatives have been undertaken towards conflict resolution. Neighbouring countries have played a vital role in mediating between Gulf states and facilitating dialogue to reduce tensions. The Sultanate of Oman, known for its diplomatic prowess and neutrality, has been an active mediator in multiple Gulf conflicts, offering a platform for negotiations and fostering dialogue between conflicting parties.

Regional organisations such as the Gulf Cooperation Council (GCC) have also sought to promote regional stability and foster cooperation between member states. The GCC's Security Pact, signed in 2000, aims to enhance collective security efforts and counterterrorism and address issues that threaten regional stability. However, Gulf conflicts have, at times, strained the unity of the organisation and highlighted the underlying divisions among its members, hindering effective resolution and cooperation.

Additionally, external powers have engaged in diplomatic efforts to mitigate Gulf conflicts and facilitate dialogue between conflicting parties. The United States, for example, has played a prominent role in brokering peace agreements and mediating disputes. The Iran nuclear deal, formally known as the Joint Comprehensive Plan of Action (JCPOA), negotiated in 2015, aimed to kerb Iran's nuclear programme and reduce tensions with Western powers, offering a glimpse of reconciliation after years of strained relations. However, the subsequent withdrawal of the United States from the agreement in 2018 has complicated diplomatic efforts and further heightened tensions in the region.

TO SUM UP

The regional implications of Gulf conflicts are multifaceted, impacting neighbouring countries, regional stability, the global economy, and the broader international order. As conflicts in the Gulf continue to evolve and intersect with existing fault lines, the need for effective conflict resolution becomes increasingly urgent. Regional and international stakeholders must work together to address the root causes of conflicts, promote dialogue, and foster a conducive environment for lasting peace and stability. Resolving Gulf conflicts will benefit not only the region but also the world. Still, it will also contribute to a more secure, prosperous, and interconnected world.

7

Transregional Issues and Conflict Resolution in the Gulf

In today's interconnected world, transregional issues have become significant challenges for countries around the globe. As the Gulf countries continue to play a crucial role in regional dynamics, addressing transregional issues and exploring effective conflict resolution strategies is essential. This chapter focuses on the factors contributing to the Gulf region's transregional conflicts. It examines potential approaches to resolving these conflicts.

THE IMPACT OF TRANSREGIONAL ISSUES IN THE GULF

Transregional issues in the Gulf region encompass challenges beyond national boundaries, with each case leaving a unique imprint on the area. One of the most significant transregional issues is illegal migration, driven by factors such as political instability, economic disparities, and conflict in neighbouring countries. The Gulf countries often serve as transit points or destinations for migrants seeking employment, leading to complex social, financial, and security implications. The influx of migrants strains resources, puts pressure on infrastructure, and can lead to ethnic tensions. Moreover, human trafficking networks often exploit vulnerable migrants, causing immense human suffering.

Another pressing concern is drug trafficking, which permeates the Gulf region due to its strategic location between drug-producing countries and major markets. Illicit drugs, such as heroin, cannabis, and amphetamines, flow through the region, nourishing criminal networks and perpetuating violence and instability. The illegal drug trade not only fuels addiction and related health issues but also undermines societal well-being and disrupts economic development. Countering drug trafficking requires multi-faceted strategies involving intelligence-sharing, joint law enforcement efforts, and international cooperation.

Additionally, terrorism remains a persistent transregional threat in the Gulf region. Extremist ideologies, often propagated online, have the potential to radicalise individuals and inspire terrorist acts. Various extremist groups have targeted the Gulf countries due to their strategic position, wealth, and influence. Addressing these security challenges necessitates a comprehensive approach, encompassing counter-terrorism efforts and deradicalisation programmes and addressing the underlying socioeconomic and political grievances that breed extremist ideologies.

UNDERSTANDING THE ROOT CAUSES

To effectively address transregional conflicts in the Gulf, it is crucial to comprehend the root causes. Socioeconomic disparities, political instability, and weak governance systems contribute to the emergence and perpetuation of transregional conflicts. Gulf countries vary in wealth distribution, with some grappling with high levels of poverty and unemployment. This disparity often leads to social tensions and creates an environment ripe for exploitation by criminal and extremist organisations.

Political instability in neighbouring countries, civil wars, and ethnic and sectarian conflicts exacerbate the transregional challenges faced by the Gulf countries. The spillover effects of conflicts in Syria, Iraq, and Yemen have had a profound impact on regional stability, with displaced populations seeking refuge and economic opportunities in the Gulf. Weak governance systems, corruption, and ineffective border control mechanisms further compound these challenges, making the Gulf region vulnerable to transregional issues.

COLLABORATIVE APPROACHES TO CONFLICT RESOLUTION

Resolving transregional conflicts in the Gulf requires co-operative efforts within the region and with external actors. Regional organisations, such as the Gulf Cooperation Council (GCC), are vital in facilitating dialogue and mediation among member states. These organisations can create platforms for constructive engagement and foster trust among Gulf countries to address shared challenges. The GCC's Joint Security Agreement and initiatives like the GCC Police Force demonstrate collective efforts to combat transregional issues.

Additionally, collaboration with external actors, such as the United Nations and neighbouring countries, can provide valuable expertise and resources in conflict resolution efforts. The international community can facilitate dialogue, provide technical assistance, and support capacity-building efforts in the Gulf countries. Neighbouring countries like Iran and Iraq can collaborate on border control measures, intelligence sharing, and joint operations to address shared security threats.

CAPACITY BUILDING AND INFORMATION SHARING

Building regional capacity and promoting information sharing are key elements in effectively addressing transregional conflicts. Enhancing border control measures, including technology-based surveillance systems, human resources training, and intelligence-sharing networks, can help combat illegal migration and drug trafficking. Coordinated efforts to dismantle human trafficking networks, combined with regional campaigns to raise awareness about the risks and consequences of irregular migration, can dissuade vulnerable populations from falling into the hands of traffickers.

Investing in education and vocational training programmes is vital to creating opportunities for the marginalised and reducing the allure of radical ideologies. The Gulf countries can address the grievances that underpin extremism by improving access to quality education and economic empowerment. Incorporating cultural and religious instruction into the curriculum can promote tolerance, understanding, and counter-narratives against radical ideologies.

Strengthening judicial systems and law enforcement agencies is also essential, enhancing their capacity to investigate and prosecute transregional criminal activities effectively. Mutual legal assistance agreements among Gulf countries and with international partners can streamline the sharing of evidence, extradition processes, and asset recovery efforts. The Gulf countries can enhance their ability to tackle transregional challenges by developing specialised units and improving cross-border co-operation.

TO SUM UP

Transregional issues pose complex challenges in the Gulf region, but they also provide opportunities for collaboration and shared solutions. The Gulf countries can effectively address transregional conflicts by understanding the root causes of these issues, embracing a cooperative approach to conflict resolution, and investing in capacity building and information sharing. Overcoming these challenges will require sustained commitment and collective action. Still, the region's stability, security, and prosperity are worth pursuing. The Gulf countries, in collaboration with regional and international partners, have the potential to create a safer and more prosperous future for their citizens and contribute to regional peace and stability.

8

Conflict Resolution Initiatives in Wider Regional Conflicts

In the tumultuous region of the Gulf, conflict resolution initiatives extend beyond the borders of individual states and encompass broader regional conflicts. This chapter delves deeper into the various approaches taken by Gulf countries in addressing and mediating disputes in neighbouring countries, highlighting the challenges faced and the successes achieved. Gulf countries play a significant role in fostering a more peaceful and prosperous region by actively engaging in diplomatic efforts, supporting international initiatives, and collaborating with other states. However, the complexity of these conflicts, compounded by geopolitical rivalries and divergent interests, presents many challenges that must be comprehensively addressed for sustainable peace.

1. CONFLICT RESOLUTION EFFORTS IN SYRIA

One significant example of conflict resolution initiatives in the Gulf involves the crisis in Syria. Gulf states, including Saudi Arabia, Qatar, and the United Arab Emirates, have been actively involved in supporting various factions within the Syrian conflict, each with their own interests and agendas. While some Gulf states have supported rebel groups seeking to overthrow the Syrian government, others have maintained diplomatic relations with the government itself. This diversity of positions has often hindered the effectiveness of conflict resolution efforts, with Gulf countries finding it difficult to reach a consensus.

Despite these challenges, Gulf countries have also engaged in multilateral efforts to address the Syrian conflict. For instance, they have actively participated in international conferences and initiatives to find a political solution and end the bloodshed. This includes supporting initiatives such as the Geneva peace talks and the Astana process, which have brought together various regional and international actors to seek a negotiated settlement. Furthermore, the Gulf Cooperation Council (GCC) has also played a role in facilitating dialogue between Syrian opposition groups and other stakeholders, aiming to find common ground and contribute to a peaceful resolution.

However, the complexity of the Syrian conflict and the involvement of numerous external actors have complicated conflict resolution efforts. The intervention of critical regional and international powers, including Russia, Iran, and Turkey, has further muddled the situation, leading to increased violence and fragmentation. Gulf countries must navigate these intricate dynamics through sustained diplomatic efforts, mediation, and dialogue, focusing on fostering inclusive negotiations and consensus-building among all parties involved.

2. ADDRESSING CONFLICT IN LIBYA

Another regional conflict that Gulf countries have sought to address is the ongoing crisis in Libya. Gulf states have historically supported different factions within the Libyan conflict, often exacerbating divisions and prolonging instability. However, in recent years, there has been a growing recognition among Gulf countries of the need for a peaceful resolution in Libya. Efforts have been made to bring together rival factions and encourage dialogue. However, progress has needed to be faster and improved in the complex dynamics of the conflict.

Gulf states have collaborated with regional and international actors, including the United Nations, to support diplomatic efforts in Libya. The Gulf countries actively participated in conferences and initiatives, such as the Berlin Conference, to find a political solution and end the country's violence. Furthermore, they have provided humanitarian aid and contributed to stabilisation efforts, recognising that sustainable conflict resolution goes hand in hand with addressing the country's underlying economic and social challenges.

One significant challenge in resolving the Libyan conflict is the involvement of external actors, each supporting different factions and pursuing their own strategic interests. These external interventions have fuelled the conflict, deepened divisions, and impeded genuine reconciliation efforts. Gulf countries must utilise their diplomatic channels and leverage their relationships with external actors to encourage them to prioritise a political solution, respect Libya's sovereignty, and support inclusive dialogue among Libyans themselves.

3. MULTI-DIMENSIONAL CHALLENGES AND COLLABORATIVE APPROACHES

In addition to specific conflicts, Gulf countries have recognised the importance of addressing broader regional issues that significantly impact their stability and security. These include challenges such as terrorism, drug trafficking, and illegal migration, which transcend national borders and require collaborative approaches for resolution.

Gulf states have actively engaged in international counter-terrorism efforts, sharing intelligence, coordinating security operations, and implementing joint initiatives to combat extremist groups. Recognising the need for comprehensive solutions, they have also focused on addressing the root causes of terrorism, promoting education, economic development, and social integration to prevent the rise of radical ideologies. Moreover, they have engaged in capacity-building and training programmes to enhance the capabilities of regional security forces in tackling terrorism.

Moreover, drug trafficking poses a significant challenge in the Gulf region, with its strategic location providing a transit route for drug smuggling. Gulf countries have intensified their cooperation with international partners, enhancing maritime security by conducting joint patrols, exchanging information, and bolstering law enforcement capabilities to intercept drug shipments. Additionally, collaborative efforts have been undertaken to disrupt the networks involved in human trafficking and irregular migration, aiming to protect vulnerable individuals while ensuring regional security. Such initiatives have involved coordination with neighbouring countries, international organisations, and non-governmental organisations to foster regional cooperation in addressing these complex transnational challenges.

4. CHALLENGES AND LESSONS LEARNT

While Gulf countries have made notable efforts in conflict resolution initiatives within broader regional conflicts, numerous challenges persist. The complexity of these conflicts, geopolitical rivalries among regional and international actors, and divergent interests of involved parties pose significant hurdles to achieving sustainable peace.

One crucial challenge is the need for more trust and deep-seated animosities between conflicting parties, often hindering dialogue and compromise. Gulf countries must employ effective confidence-building measures and mediation processes and track two diplomatic channels to foster trust among the warring factions and create an environment conducive to negotiations.

Achieving consensus among Gulf countries and other stakeholders with varying positions on particular conflicts remains challenging. Gulf states must continue fostering diplomatic dialogue, engaging in quiet diplomacy, and seeking common ground to bridge their differences and enhance cooperation. Moreover, strengthening regional alliances, such as the Gulf Cooperation Council, can provide a platform for Gulf countries to present a united front and jointly advocate for conflict resolution and regional stability.

TO SUM UP

Resolution initiatives in broader regional conflicts are crucial to the Gulf countries' efforts to promote peace and stability. The Gulf states' active involvement in diplomatic efforts, support of international initiatives, and collaboration with other states underscore their commitment to addressing conflicts beyond their borders. While challenges persist, these efforts demonstrate a dedication to fostering a more peaceful and prosperous region. By continuing to navigate the complexities, Gulf countries have the potential to make substantial contributions to conflict resolution in broader regional conflicts. Through sustained diplomacy, mediation, and dialogue, they can forge paths towards sustainable peace, regional cooperation, and the well-being of people in the wider Gulf region.

9

Case Study (1)

NATIONAL RECONCILIATION
PROCESSES IN IRAQ

In the wake of the US invasion of Iraq in 2003 and the subsequent toppling of Saddam Hussein's regime, the country was thrust into a period of intense instability and sectarian violence. The deep divisions between different ethnic and religious groups within Iraq, namely the Sunni Arabs, Shia Arabs, and Kurds, exacerbated tensions and fuelled a cycle of violence, creating significant challenges for political stability and societal cohesion. The Iraqi government and various stakeholders initiated national reconciliation processes to address these divisions and forge a more inclusive and united Iraq.

BACKGROUND OF ETHNIC AND RELIGIOUS DIVISIONS

To understand the significance and complexity of the national reconciliation processes in Iraq, it is crucial to examine the historical context of the country's profound ethnic and religious divisions. Iraq's population is primarily divided into three main groups: the Sunni Arabs, who were the dominant group under Saddam Hussein's regime; the Shia Arabs, who make up the majority of the population; and the Kurds, who inhabit the northern region of the country and have long sought autonomy.

Under Saddam Hussein, Iraq experienced a brutal dictatorship that systematically marginalised and oppressed certain groups. Saddam's regime mainly targeted the Kurdish population in the north and the Shia Arabs, who were often viewed as a threat to his Sunni-dominated regime. This led to deep-seated grievances and a sense of exclusion among these communities. Furthermore, the sectarian nature of politics under Saddam fostered a culture of mistrust and hatred between Sunni and Shia Arabs, which would later fuel violence in the post-Saddam era.

THE NEED FOR NATIONAL RECONCILIATION

In the aftermath of Saddam Hussein's regime, Iraq faced numerous challenges in terms of political stability and societal cohesion. Sectarian violence between Sunni and Shia communities, along with the aspirations of Kurdish autonomy, threatened to plunge the country into a full-blown civil war. It became imperative for Iraq to undergo a comprehensive national reconciliation process to address these divisions, heal wounds, and establish a framework for a more inclusive and united country.

INITIATION OF THE NATIONAL RECONCILIATION PROCESSES

The national reconciliation processes in Iraq were multifaceted. They involved various actors such as political leaders, community representatives, and international organisations. One notable initiative was the Shia-led government's attempt to reach out to Sunni Arab groups and integrate them into the political process. This involved offering amnesty to former Baath Party members and engaging in dialogue with Sunni leaders. Similarly, efforts were made to address the aspirations of the Kurdish population through negotiations on power-sharing and autonomy in the north.

The Shia-led government, under Prime Minister Nouri al-Maliki, recognised the critical importance of engaging with Sunni Arab groups and addressing their grievances. The initiation of national reconciliation processes was marked by establishing the Iraqi High Commission for National Reconciliation in 2004, tasked with promoting dialogue and reconciliation among different communities. This commission facilitated direct negotiations between critical stakeholders. It encouraged the participation of Sunni Arab political leaders in the political process.

CHALLENGES AND OBSTACLES

The national reconciliation processes in Iraq faced significant challenges and obstacles along the way. The deep-rooted mistrust and hatred between different ethnic and religious groups forged over decades of oppression and violence hindered progress. Additionally, the widespread violence and insurgency in the aftermath of Saddam Hussein's regime posed a constant threat to stability and the success of reconciliation efforts.

Extremist groups such as Al-Qaeda in Iraq and later the Islamic State (IS) emerged and capitalised on the sectarian divisions, further exacerbating tensions and undermining the reconciliation processes. These groups sought to exploit Sunni grievances and marginalisation to recruit supporters and fuel sectarian violence. The terrorist attacks conducted by these groups not only targeted Shia communities but also inflicted significant harm on Sunni civilians, perpetuating fear and suspicion among communities.

Moreover, external factors and interventions complicated the reconciliation processes. Iraq's sectarian divisions were often fuelled by regional powers seeking to exert influence and advance their interests. Iran, a predominantly Shia country, supported Shia groups in Iraq. In contrast, countries such as Saudi

Arabia and Turkey extended support to Sunni Arab factions. These external interventions exacerbated existing tensions and made the reconciliation processes more challenging.

OUTCOMES AND IMPACT

While the national reconciliation processes in Iraq faced significant challenges, they did yield some positive outcomes and have had a lasting impact on the country. Integrating Sunni Arab groups into the political process helped reduce violence and encouraged Sunni participation in governance. This, in turn, fostered a sense of inclusion and representation among Sunni communities. The establishment of power-sharing mechanisms, as enshrined in the 2010 National Partnership Agreement, contributed to improved relations between the central government and the Kurdistan Regional Government, addressing Kurdish aspirations and further stabilising the country.

Furthermore, the reconciliation efforts helped pave the way for a more inclusive political system and constitutional reforms. The new Iraqi constitution, adopted in 2005, recognised the rights of ethnic and religious minorities and enshrined principles of power-sharing and federalism. This provided a framework for addressing the concerns of various communities and ensuring their representation in the political process.

LESSONS LEARNT

The case of national reconciliation processes in Iraq offers several critical lessons for conflict resolution initiatives in other contexts. It highlights the importance of inclusivity, dialogue, and compromise in addressing deep-rooted divisions. Engaging different ethnic and religious groups and key stakeholders is crucial for creating a sense of ownership and legitimacy in reconciliation. This can be achieved by establishing formal institutions, such as the Iraqi High Commission for National Reconciliation, which bring together representatives from different communities and foster dialogue.

The case of Iraq also emphasises the need for sustained international support and engagement to ensure the success and sustainability of reconciliation efforts. The international community can play a critical role in providing technical assistance, mediating negotiations, and creating an enabling environment for dialogue. Additionally, international actors should be mindful of regional dynamics and potential external interventions that could undermine reconciliation processes.

TO SUM UP

The national reconciliation processes in Iraq have played a significant role in addressing the deep divisions and conflicts that emerged after the fall of Saddam Hussein's regime. While the road to reconciliation has been arduous and fraught with challenges, these processes have contributed to reducing violence, fostering inclusivity, and establishing a framework for a more united Iraq. The lessons learnt from this case study can inform and inspire conflict resolution efforts in other regions facing similar reconciliation challenges. Recognising the importance of dialogue, inclusivity, and sustained international support makes navigating complex and deeply divided societies towards a more peaceful and inclusive future possible.

10

Women's Roles in Conflict Resolution

In recent years, there has been a growing recognition of the vital role that women can play in conflict resolution processes. Traditionally marginalised and excluded from decision-making spaces, women have unique perspectives and contributions that can significantly impact conflict resolution efforts. This chapter delves deeper into the importance of women's roles in conflict resolution. It explores how their participation can lead to more sustainable and inclusive outcomes.

1. THE POWER OF INCLUSION

Including women in conflict resolution processes is not just a matter of gender equality but also a strategic imperative. Research has consistently shown that peace agreements and sustainable solutions are more likely to be achieved when women are actively involved in negotiations and decision-making. The United Nations Security Council resolution 1325, passed in 2000, was a landmark step in recognising women's crucial roles in peacebuilding and the need for their participation at all levels of conflict resolution.

Women bring different experiences, perspectives, and priorities to the table, which can broaden the scope of discussions and result in more comprehensive and durable solutions. By foregrounding women's agency and expertise, their involvement ensures that peacebuilding efforts address a more extensive range of concerns, including socio-economic disparities, environmental sustainability, and the protection and promotion of human rights. Their inclusion challenges the status quo and disrupts power dynamics that perpetuate conflict, leading to more transformative peace processes.

2. BUILDING TRUST AND SOCIAL COHESION

Women often play critical roles in building and maintaining community social networks. These networks can establish trust, facilitate dialogue, and foster social cohesion in conflict-affected areas. Women's relational strengths and empathy enable them to bridge divides, unite diverse stakeholders, and lay the groundwork for sustainable peacebuilding processes.

Women's relationships and connections span not only within their immediate communities but also across ethnic, religious, and cultural boundaries. As connectors and mediators, women can transcend the divisions created by conflict and work towards healing and reconciliation. Their grassroots engagement enables them to understand community members' nuanced needs and concerns, allowing for more targeted conflict resolution strategies that address root causes individually and collectively.

3. MEDIATING COMMUNITY-LEVEL CONFLICTS

While formal peace negotiations often receive the most attention, community-level conflicts and tensions also demand attention to prevent further escalation. Due to their deep understanding of local dynamics and close ties within communities, women can effectively mediate and address these conflicts at the grassroots level. Women's participation in conflict resolution is more comprehensive than structured processes in many contexts. Still, it extends to day-to-day problem-solving and peacebuilding initiatives.

Women's involvement can provide an alternative approach to conflict resolution, focusing on community healing, restoration, and reconciliation. They often employ storytelling, dialogue circles, and transformative justice methods to address underlying grievances and promote mutual understanding. Women can influence decision-making processes, challenge aggression, and contribute to transforming conflict dynamics by working closely with affected individuals and groups. Their emphasis on inclusivity, empathy, and participatory approaches often results in more sustainable and locally-owned resolutions.

4. TRANSFORMING GENDER NORMS AND POWER RELATIONS

Women's participation challenges and transforms gender norms and power relations that contribute to the perpetuation of conflicts. Women's involvement in decision-making processes disrupts traditional hierarchical structures and fosters a more inclusive and egalitarian approach to conflict resolution. By actively shaping peace processes, women challenge patriarchal norms, stereotypes, and biases that marginalise them and perpetuate inequalities.

Moreover, women's participation fosters a culture of nonviolence and empathy, promoting alternative forms of masculinity and challenging toxic masculinity that perpetuates violence. As agents of change, they inspire and mobilise others, including men, to challenge oppressive systems and work towards gender equality. The transformation of gender norms within conflict resolution processes leads to more inclusive outcomes. It contributes to creating long-term sustainable peace and justice in society.

5. ADVANCING GENDER-SENSITIVE APPROACHES TO CONFLICT RESOLUTION

Gender-sensitive conflict resolution processes are more likely to address root causes and create lasting peace. Women's participation ensures that gendered impacts and perspectives are considered, challenging patriarchal norms and enabling the development of more inclusive policies and programmes. By actively involving women, conflict resolution initiatives can advance gender equality and women's empowerment during and after conflicts.

In addition to ensuring women's meaningful participation, gender-sensitive approaches require integrating gender analysis into conflict assessments and designating resources towards addressing gendered needs. Addressing women's and marginalised groups' specific needs and priorities, such as access to justice, healthcare, education, and economic opportunities, is crucial in post-conflict reconstruction and sustainable development. By placing women's lived experiences at the centre of conflict analysis and resolution, gender-sensitive approaches can help transform unequal power dynamics and promote social justice.

6. OVERCOMING BARRIERS AND CHALLENGES

Despite the recognised importance of women's roles in conflict resolution, numerous barriers persist. Discriminatory societal norms, limited access to resources and education, cultural restrictions, and institutional biases often hinder women's meaningful participation. Efforts must be made to remove these obstacles and create enabling environments that promote and protect women's rights and participation.

Ensuring women's inclusion requires engaging with multiple stakeholders, including civil society organisations, religious and community leaders, and governments. Building awareness and providing training on gender equality, conflict resolution, and human rights are crucial to increase the pool of women leaders and enable their meaningful participation. Addressing gender stereotypes and biases within institutions is necessary to create more inclusive spaces for women in decision-making processes.

TO SUM UP

Women have a significant role to play in conflict resolution processes. Their inclusion brings diverse perspectives, builds trust, mediates community-level conflicts, transforms gender norms, and advances gender-sensitive approaches. Recognising and harnessing these contributions is essential for sustainable peace, social justice, and achieving the United Nations' Sustainable Development Goals.

By actively involving women in conflict resolution, we can create more inclusive, comprehensive, and enduring solutions that benefit all members of society. Women's experiences and expertise must be valued, respected, and integrated into all aspects of conflict resolution efforts. We can only realise the full potential of inclusive and lasting peace in our world by embracing their diverse contributions.

11

Case Study (2)

YEMEN'S ROAD TO RECONCILIATION

Yemen has been embroiled in a devastating civil war since 2014, when the Houthi rebels seized control of the capital, Sana'a, and forced the internationally recognised government into exile. This conflict has unleashed a humanitarian crisis of immense proportions, with millions of Yemenis suffering from food insecurity, displacement, and limited access to essential services.

The road to reconciliation in Yemen has been long and arduous, characterised by failed peace talks and ceasefire attempts. However, amidst this challenging landscape, significant developments and initiatives offer glimpses of hope for a sustainable resolution to the conflict, even though countless obstacles continue to hamper progress.

One of the most critical milestones in Yemen's path to reconciliation was the Stockholm Agreement, reached in December 2018 between the warring parties. This groundbreaking agreement aimed to establish a framework for peace in Yemen and included provisions such as a ceasefire in the strategic port city of Hodeidah, a vital lifeline for humanitarian aid, and establishing a joint committee responsible for overseeing the withdrawal of forces from the city.

While the Stockholm Agreement provided a temporary respite and garnered international attention, implementing its provisions proved challenging. Both sides accused each other of violating the ceasefire, and progress in withdrawing forces from Hodeidah was slow and contentious. The agreement did, however, demonstrate that dialogue and negotiation were possible, even amidst deep-rooted animosities.

Another critical step in Yemen's journey towards reconciliation was the establishment of the Redeployment Coordination Committee (RCC) under the auspices of the United Nations. This committee, composed of representatives from the Yemeni government and the Houthi rebels, was tasked with overseeing the redeployment of forces from Hodeidah and other strategic locations.

Although the RCC faced considerable obstacles and setbacks, it managed to facilitate the initial redeployment of forces from Hodeidah, thereby alleviating some of the concerns regarding the flow of humanitarian aid. This achievement highlighted the importance of sustained diplomatic efforts and third-party mediation in building trust and fostering cooperation between the conflicting parties.

In addition to these formal peace initiatives, local reconciliation efforts have played a crucial role in Yemen's path towards resolving the conflict. In several areas of the country, tribal leaders, religious figures, and civil society activists have engaged in grassroots reconciliation initiatives, bringing communities together to address grievances and build bridges between factions.

These local reconciliation processes have demonstrated the importance of inclusivity, dialogue, and addressing the root causes of the conflict at the community level. They have helped counter the divisive rhetoric propagated by the warring parties and fostered a sense of shared identity and common goals among Yemenis, transcending sectarian and regional differences.

Furthermore, international actors have been actively involved in supporting Yemen's reconciliation efforts. The United Nations has played a significant role in facilitating negotiations, providing technical assistance, and coordinating humanitarian aid through its various agencies and Special Envoy for Yemen. Additionally, regional powers such as Saudi Arabia, Iran, and the United Arab Emirates have been involved in mediation attempts. However, their interests and rivalry have sometimes complicated the peace process.

However, despite these encouraging developments, Yemen's path to reconciliation continues to face daunting challenges. The deep-seated mistrust between the warring parties, the proliferation of armed groups, and the underlying economic and political grievances that fuelled the conflict persist. The humanitarian crisis has worsened due to economic deterioration, the COVID-19 pandemic, and limited access to essential services such as clean water and healthcare.

Sustained international pressure and support for Yemen's peace process are crucial to overcoming these obstacles. This includes ensuring the provision of essential humanitarian aid, working towards a nationwide ceasefire, empowering local reconciliation processes, and addressing the underlying causes of the conflict, such as political representation and economic disparities.

Yemen's road to reconciliation can be further facilitated by learning from the successes and failures of previous conflict resolution initiatives. Encouragingly, the international community continues to rally behind this cause, recognising the urgent need to end the suffering of the Yemeni people and pave the way for a peaceful and prosperous future.

Efforts to address the humanitarian crisis are also of paramount importance. The Yemeni people are facing severe food shortages, malnutrition, and the destruction of critical infrastructure. The international community must continue to provide humanitarian aid and work towards stabilising the situation, ensuring that the most vulnerable populations receive the necessary assistance.

Furthermore, broader political dialogue is needed to address the underlying social, economic, and political grievances that have fuelled the conflict. This includes facilitating inclusive discussions on power sharing, equitable resource distribution, and democratic reforms.

International actors should also continue to promote accountability for human rights abuses and violations committed during the conflict. The establishment of a credible and impartial mechanism to investigate and prosecute war crimes is essential for ensuring justice and preventing impunity.

Moreover, rebuilding Yemen's economy is essential for long-term stability and reconciliation. The war has devastated the country's infrastructure and disrupted economic activities. It is crucial to prioritise reconstruction and create sustainable livelihood opportunities for Yemenis, reducing their reliance on external aid and fostering economic resilience.

To sum up, Yemen's road to reconciliation is fraught with challenges. Still, the progress made through initiatives such as the Stockholm Agreement, the RCC, and local reconciliation efforts offer glimpses of hope. With continued international support and sustained diplomatic efforts, a durable peace in Yemen is not only possible but is essential for the well-being and future of this war-weary nation. Efforts should be intensified to address the humanitarian crisis, foster political dialogue, promote accountability, and rebuild Yemen's economy. Only through a comprehensive and holistic approach can Yemen overcome the legacy of conflict and move towards a brighter and more prosperous future.

12

Peacebuilding Through Education and Cultural Exchange

Exploring diverse peacebuilding avenues is crucial in pursuing lasting peace and stability in the Gulf region. While political negotiations and diplomatic efforts play a significant role, the power of education and cultural exchange should not be underestimated. This chapter delves into the potential of these two factors in fostering understanding, empathy, and mutual respect between countries and communities within the Gulf.

THE IMPORTANCE OF EDUCATION

Formal and informal education is vital in building a culture of peace. By promoting inclusive and comprehensive educational systems, nations can cultivate values such as tolerance, respect for diversity, and conflict resolution skills. This can be achieved through various means, including curriculum reforms, promoting civic education, and teaching conflict resolution techniques from an early age.

Educational reforms have been a critical component of peacebuilding efforts in the Gulf region. Countries have recognised the significance of teaching history in an unbiased manner, acknowledging past conflicts, and seeking to build a shared narrative that fosters empathy and reconciliation. By incorporating multiple perspectives into history textbooks and ensuring a balanced portrayal of historical events, educational institutions can help prevent the perpetuation of grievances and the deepening of divisions.

Additionally, educational institutions can be crucial in addressing the root causes of conflict and social inequality. By focusing on topics such as human rights, gender equality, sustainable development, and environmental stewardship, students can develop a holistic understanding of the interconnectedness between peace, justice, and social progress. These fundamental values align with the United Nations Sustainable Development Goals (SDGs) and provide a framework for integrating peacebuilding principles into educational curricula.

Civic education is another critical aspect of peacebuilding through education. By teaching students about their rights and responsibilities as citizens and the importance of active participation in democratic processes, educational institutions contribute to the development of a well-informed and engaged citizenry. This empowers individuals to peacefully voice their concerns, resolve disputes, and advocate for positive community change.

Beyond traditional classroom education, extracurricular activities that promote intercultural understanding and cooperation play a significant role. Model United Nations conferences, global citizenship programmes, and community service initiatives encourage students to work together on common goals, fostering respect and empathy for diverse perspectives. These experiences enhance students' understanding of global issues and equip them with invaluable critical thinking, communication, and collaboration skills.

Moreover, incorporating peace education into teacher training programmes is crucial. By equipping educators with the knowledge and tools to facilitate dialogue, encourage critical thinking, and address conflict constructively, they become agents of peace within their classrooms and communities. Teacher training programmes also emphasise creating inclusive learning environments that embrace diversity, challenge stereotypes, and promote intercultural understanding.

CULTURAL EXCHANGE AS A BRIDGE

Cultural exchange programmes present another avenue for peacebuilding in the Gulf. By facilitating interactions and fostering understanding between people from different countries and cultures, these programmes offer a platform for dialogue and cooperation.

Through cultural exchanges, individuals can dispel stereotypes, overcome prejudices, and develop a deeper appreciation for each other's traditions, languages, and customs. These experiences help build empathy, and highlight shared values and aspirations.

Initiatives such as student exchange programmes, art and music festivals, and sports events encourage interactions that transcend boundaries and promote harmony. By collaborating on various cultural projects, nations within the Gulf can foster trust and create a sense of shared identity.

Partnerships with international organisations, NGOs, and cultural institutions can strengthen these initiatives. By leveraging their expertise, resources, and networks, countries in the Gulf can expand the impact of cultural exchange programmes and amplify the message of peace and understanding.

Furthermore, digital platforms and technology can be vital in promoting cultural exchange in the Gulf. Virtual exchange programmes, online language learning platforms, and digital storytelling projects allow individuals to connect, share experiences, and foster mutual understanding. Leveraging these technological advancements can ensure more comprehensive access to cultural exchange opportunities and overcome limitations posed by travel restrictions or resource constraints.

Cultural exchange programmes can promote cultural understanding and focus on economic cooperation. By encouraging entrepreneurship, trade, and joint ventures, nations in the Gulf can create economic interdependence, fostering a shared interest in peace and stability. Economic cooperation can help build trust, reinforce intercultural relationships, and dismantle barriers that hinder peaceful collaboration.

CHALLENGES AND OPPORTUNITIES

Implementing peacebuilding through education and cultural exchange initiatives is challenging. Overcoming political tensions, language barriers, and logistical issues can be daunting. Moreover, cultural biases and historical grievances may impede progress. However, with strong leadership, commitment, and collaboration, these challenges can be addressed and turned into opportunities for growth and reconciliation.

Ensuring inclusivity and representation within educational and cultural exchange programmes is challenging. It is crucial to provide opportunities for participants from marginalised communities, different socioeconomic backgrounds, and minorities to engage and benefit from these initiatives actively. By promoting diversity and inclusivity, these programmes can contribute to reducing inequality and strengthening social cohesion.

Another challenge lies in evaluating and monitoring the impact of these initiatives. It is crucial to develop robust frameworks and methodologies to assess the effectiveness of peacebuilding through education and cultural exchange. Regular monitoring, feedback mechanisms, and continuous learning will help refine approaches, identify best practices, and ensure sustained positive impact.

TO SUM UP

Peacebuilding through education and cultural exchange is essential to creating sustainable peace in the Gulf region. Nations can gradually break down barriers by investing in quality education systems that foster tolerance and conflict resolution skills and promote cultural exchange programmes that encourage dialogue and understanding. These initiatives can transform mindsets, bridge divides, and foster peaceful coexistence in the Gulf.

Through collaborative efforts, using technology as an enabler, and ensuring inclusivity, the impact of peacebuilding through education and cultural exchange can extend beyond borders, contributing to a more harmonious and prosperous future for the Gulf region. These initiatives can lay the foundation for a generation of individuals who embrace diversity, respect human rights, and actively work towards a shared vision of peace and stability. In the face of complex challenges, education and cultural exchange are potent tools to shape a brighter future for the Gulf.

13

Oman as Mediator

Over the years, Oman has emerged as a key player in mediating conflicts within the Gulf region. It has played a pivotal role in facilitating reconciliation between feuding Gulf countries. Oman's unique neutral and trusted mediator position has allowed it to navigate complex political landscapes successfully and bring warring factions to the negotiating table. This chapter deeply explores Oman's significant contributions to mediating Gulf country reconciliations and highlights the key factors that have made Oman an effective mediator.

1. THE TRADITION OF NEUTRALITY

Oman's longstanding tradition of neutrality in regional conflicts has been a cornerstone of its mediation efforts. Unlike some other Gulf countries, Oman has consistently maintained a balanced approach, refraining from taking sides and instead focusing on promoting dialogue and understanding between conflicting parties. This neutrality has not only earned Oman the trust of various factions. Still, it has also allowed the country to act as an honest broker, facilitating negotiations in a genuinely impartial manner. Oman's ability to set aside its political interests and prioritise peaceful resolutions has been crucial in gaining the respect and cooperation of warring parties.

2. SULTAN QABOOS' DIPLOMATIC VISION

The late Sultan Qaboos bin Said, Oman's former ruler, profoundly impacted Oman's mediation efforts. He firmly believed in the power of dialogue and diplomacy to resolve conflicts, and his active involvement in mediation greatly enhanced Oman's reputation as a trusted mediator. Sultan Qaboos' relationships with leaders across the Gulf region and beyond gave him a unique ability to bridge divides and foster an environment conducive to productive negotiations. His commitment to peaceful resolutions and dedication to maintaining positive relationships with all Gulf countries were crucial in establishing Oman as a reliable mediator.

3. QUIET DIPLOMACY AND CONFIDENCE BUILDING

Oman's mediation approach has been characterised by a commitment to quiet diplomacy, emphasising confidential negotiations and trust-building measures. Recognising the sensitive nature of conflicts within the Gulf, Oman has promoted discreet and behind-the-scenes talks, allowing parties to openly discuss their grievances and concerns without the fear of public scrutiny or backlash. This approach has been particularly effective in generating an environment of trust, encouraging open and honest dialogue between parties that may otherwise have been reluctant to engage. Oman has overcome deep-rooted mistrust and facilitated constructive communication by offering a safe and confidential negotiation space.

4. UTILISING INFORMAL CHANNELS

In addition to formal diplomatic channels, Oman has leveraged informal networks and back-channel diplomacy to facilitate negotiations. Oman's ability to establish trusted relationships with key stakeholders on all sides of a conflict has provided a unique advantage in building bridges and addressing underlying tensions that hinder reconciliation efforts. These informal channels have proven effective in creating opportunities for genuine dialogue, away from the pressures and constraints of official negotiations, enabling parties to express their concerns and explore potential solutions more freely. Oman's mediators have used their relationships and networks to bridge gaps, foster mutual understanding, and generate momentum towards reconciliation.

5. EMPHASISING HUMANITARIAN CONCERNS

Oman recognises the importance of addressing humanitarian concerns as a crucial aspect of the reconciliation process. Understanding that conflicts in the Gulf region often result in significant human suffering and displacement, Oman has consistently advocated for the well-being of affected populations. By highlighting the urgency of addressing these humanitarian crises and advocating for their alleviation, Oman has motivated parties to prioritise resolving their differences and finding common ground for their people's greater good. Oman's emphasis on the human impact of conflicts has been instrumental in encouraging parties to move beyond their differences and work together to build a more stable future.

6. PROMOTING SUSTAINABLE SOLUTIONS

Oman's mediation efforts go beyond mere conflict management. The country firmly believes in achieving sustainable solutions that address the root causes of conflicts and pave the way for long-term stability and cooperation across the Gulf region. Rather than focusing solely on temporary ceasefires or quick fixes, Oman encourages parties to engage in comprehensive dialogue, compromise, and reconciliation. By seeking to resolve underlying grievances and fostering a shared vision for the future, Oman's mediation aims to establish a solid foundation for lasting peace. This long-term approach acknowledges the complexities of the conflicts. It seeks to address their underlying causes to prevent further disputes from arising.

7. LESSONS LEARNT AND FUTURE OUTLOOK

Oman's success in mediating Gulf country reconciliations provides valuable lessons for conflict resolution initiatives in the region and beyond. The country's experience underscores the importance of commitment, impartiality, and diplomacy in resolving protracted conflicts. In conjunction with utilising informal channels, the quiet and confidential diplomacy approach has proven effective in building trust and fostering open dialogue. Furthermore, Oman's emphasis on addressing humanitarian concerns and promoting sustainable solutions highlights the holistic nature of its mediation efforts. Oman's role in mediation is expected to remain prominent as the Gulf region faces ongoing challenges and opportunities for peaceful resolutions. As conflicts within the Gulf evolve, Oman's mediation model can serve as a blueprint for other countries seeking to foster reconciliation and build sustainable peace.

In summary, Oman's role in mediating Gulf country reconciliations is characterised by its commitment to neutrality, Sultan Qaboos's diplomatic vision, quiet diplomacy, and informal channel use. By emphasising humanitarian concerns and promoting sustainable solutions, Oman's mediation efforts have contributed significantly to fostering peace and stability in the Gulf region. Oman's experience serves as a valuable model for other countries grappling with conflicts, demonstrating the effectiveness of a balanced and inclusive approach to mediation.

14

Conflict Resolution on Transregional Issues

ILLEGAL MIGRATION, DRUG TRAFFICKING, AND TERRORISM

Illegal migration, drug trafficking, and terrorism are complex and interconnected transregional issues that have significant implications for the stability, security, and development of the Gulf region. These challenges necessitate comprehensive and collaborative efforts to find sustainable solutions safeguarding the region's and its people's well-being.

Illegal migration has been a long-standing concern in the Gulf, driven by economic disparities, political instability, and conflict in neighbouring regions. The Gulf countries have witnessed a significant influx of irregular migrants, straining available resources, creating social tensions, and posing potential security risks. Addressing illegal migration requires a multifaceted approach beyond merely treating the symptoms to tackling the underlying causes.

Cooperation between Gulf countries, countries of origin, and transit nations is essential to address the push factors leading to migration. Firstly, addressing economic disparities is crucial. Enhancing economic opportunities and job creation in countries of origin can reduce the motivation for individuals to migrate in search of better livelihoods. Gulf countries can support economic development through investment, trade partnerships, and financial support for infrastructure projects and capacity building in targeted areas.

Secondly, political stability and conflict resolution are vital for addressing migratory pressures. Active diplomacy and engagement in conflict resolution efforts by Gulf countries can contribute to regional stability and reduce the drivers of migration. Encouraging dialogue and mediation initiatives in conflict-affected regions, supporting peace initiatives, and providing humanitarian assistance to affected populations are essential steps in this regard.

Thirdly, border security and effective immigration policies are vital for managing migration flows. Gulf countries should invest in strengthening their border control mechanisms, utilising advanced technologies, and expanding their law enforcement capacities to detect and deter irregular migration. Implementing fair, efficient, and transparent immigration policies that balance security concerns with respect for human rights is essential. This includes establishing clear pathways for legal migration, such as guest worker programmes, that meet labour market demands while ensuring the protection of migrant workers' rights.

Additionally, it is crucial to invest in integration programmes and promote dialogue between host communities and migrants. Social cohesion can be fostered through language and skills training, providing access to education and healthcare, and promoting cultural exchange programmes. Addressing xenophobia and discrimination through public awareness campaigns and training for law enforcement officials can contribute to creating inclusive societies that value diversity.

Drug trafficking poses another significant transregional challenge in the Gulf. Due to its strategic location, the region has become an attractive transit route for drug smugglers, transporting narcotics from producing areas to consumer markets. The inflow of drugs not only contributes to addiction and social problems within the Gulf countries but also provides funding to criminal networks and terrorist organisations.

Combating drug trafficking requires heightened cooperation among Gulf countries, neighbouring regions, and international partners. Strengthening law enforcement agencies, enhancing intelligence-sharing mechanisms, improving border controls, and implementing effective measures to disrupt drug trafficking networks are crucial steps in resolving this issue.

Gulf countries should invest in the capacity building of their law enforcement agencies, equipping them with the necessary tools to combat drug trafficking effectively. This includes training programmes on intelligence analysis, evidence collection, and interagency cooperation. Establishing joint task forces and sharing best practices among Gulf countries can strengthen collaboration and coordination in tackling drug trafficking.

Furthermore, cooperation with neighbouring regions and international partners is essential. Sharing intelligence on drug trafficking routes, modus operandi, and financial networks can enable targeted and coordinated operations that disrupt the entire drug supply chain. Gulf countries can work closely with transit nations and governments of drug production to implement joint initiatives. These include stepped-up maritime patrols, intelligence sharing and training cooperation, and capacity-building efforts.

Additionally, investing in rehabilitation programmes, addressing social vulnerabilities, and promoting awareness campaigns can help reduce the demand for illicit drugs within the Gulf. Recognising drug addiction as a health issue rather than solely a criminal one and providing comprehensive and accessible treatment options is crucial. Prevention programmes targeting vulnerable communities, such as youth, and promoting holistic approaches involving healthcare professionals, educators, and community leaders can contribute to a reduction in drug abuse.

Terrorism remains a grave concern in the Gulf, with various extremist groups seeking to exploit regional vulnerabilities for their ideological agendas. The rise of organisations like ISIS and other terrorist entities in neighbouring regions has heightened security threats for the Gulf countries.

Resolving terrorism requires a holistic approach that addresses the issue's military, political, and socio-economic dimensions. Gulf countries have taken significant measures to counter terrorism through regional alliances such as the Gulf Cooperation Council (GCC) and international partnerships. Collaboration in intelligence sharing, joint law enforcement operations, countering financing of terrorism, and countering extremist ideologies are essential components in the fight against terrorism.

Strengthening military capabilities and coordination among Gulf countries can contribute to the active deterrence and containment of terrorist activities. Joint exercises, sharing of best practices, and developing the necessary infrastructure for rapid response and intelligence sharing can enhance the region's collective security.

Political efforts should focus on addressing factors that contribute to radicalisation and extremism. Gulf countries can prioritise countering the narrative of extremist ideologies by funding research institutions and think tanks that study and promote moderate interpretations of Islam. Inclusive political systems encouraging participation, dialogue, and respect for human rights can also help create an environment that challenges radical ideologies.

Furthermore, investing in education, promoting religious tolerance, and addressing social grievances can contribute to long-term prevention efforts against radicalisation. Integrating tolerance, respect, and coexistence values within educational curricula can help build resilient societies. Engaging religious leaders and community influencers in countering extremist narratives and promoting interfaith dialogue can foster social cohesion and prevent the spread of radical ideologies.

Resolving transregional issues such as illegal migration, drug trafficking, and terrorism necessitates not only the efforts of individual Gulf countries but also comprehensive regional and international collaboration. These interconnected challenges require a holistic and multidimensional approach that tackles root causes, strengthens institutional capacities, and fosters stakeholder collaboration. The Gulf countries should actively engage in global dialogues, sharing their experiences and expertise to contribute to broader conflict resolution efforts. By working together, the Gulf countries can effectively mitigate the impact of these transregional challenges and pave the way for a more secure and prosperous future for the region.

15

Case Study (3)

GULF STATES' CONTRIBUTIONS TO CONFLICT RESOLUTION IN SUDAN

For many years, the conflict in Sudan has been characterised by deep-rooted divisions, violence, displacement, and political instability. This chapter will delve even deeper into the Gulf states' significant and often overlooked contributions to mediating and resolving conflicts within Sudan. Their multifaceted involvement in conflict resolution processes has brought about positive changes and holds valuable lessons for future initiatives.

1. THE HISTORICAL CONTEXT OF THE CONFLICT IN SUDAN

To understand the Gulf states' complex role in conflict resolution in Sudan, it is essential to provide a comprehensive historical context of the conflict. The conflict in Sudan can be traced back to the colonial period when the British introduced policies that fuelled tensions among ethnic and religious groups. After gaining independence in 1956, Sudan struggled with power struggles, marginalisation, and the exploitation of resources. The longstanding tensions between Sudan's government and different rebel groups, primarily from Darfur, Southern Sudan, and the Blue Nile region, have perpetuated the conflict. This chapter will explore the complexities of the competition to underscore the crucial need for mediation.

2. THE GCC'S MEDIATION EFFORTS

The Gulf Cooperation Council (GCC), a regional organisation comprised of Bahrain, Kuwait, Oman, Qatar, Saudi Arabia, and the United Arab Emirates (UAE), has played a pivotal role in the conflict resolution process in Sudan. Their involvement has been multifaceted, involving diplomatic efforts and substantial financial aid. Recognising the destructive nature of the conflict in Sudan, the GCC has sought to uphold its commitment to peace and stability in the region.

2.1 Diplomatic Initiatives and Mediation

The Gulf states have actively engaged in diplomatic initiatives and mediation to resolve the conflict in Sudan. One noteworthy example is the role of Qatari diplomacy in mediating peace talks between the Sudanese government and rebel groups, leading to the signing of the Doha Document for Peace in Darfur in 2011. The Qatari government facilitated negotiations, provided a neutral ground for dialogue, and committed financial resources to support the peace process. The success of the Doha Document demonstrates the effectiveness of regional actors as mediators in complex conflicts.

Furthermore, the GCC has consistently supported regional and international efforts, such as the African Union-led mediation process, to bring all stakeholders to the negotiating table and facilitate comprehensive peace agreements. The Gulf states have provided logistical and financial support to peace talks, ensuring the participation of key actors, including the Sudanese government, rebel groups, and civil society organisations. Their interventions have helped bridge divides, foster trust, and promote inclusive dialogue.

2.2 Humanitarian Aid and Financial Contributions

The Gulf states, particularly Saudi Arabia and the UAE, have significantly contributed to Sudan to support conflict resolution and post-conflict reconstruction efforts. These contributions have addressed immediate and long-term needs, including humanitarian aid, infrastructure development, and economic support. Recognising that sustainable peace cannot be achieved without addressing the underlying social and economic drivers of conflict, the Gulf states have invested heavily in education, healthcare, and job creation programmes.

Their financial aid has helped conflict-affected populations rebuild trust between conflicting parties. By focusing on long-term development and addressing socioeconomic disparities, the Gulf states' contributions have aimed to create an enabling environment for sustainable peace to take hold. They have prioritised projects that improve access to essential services, promote social cohesion, and support livelihood opportunities for marginalised communities.

3. THE ROLE OF BILATERAL RELATIONS

Bilateral relations between the Gulf states and Sudan have also played a crucial role in conflict resolution efforts. The close ties between the Gulf states and Sudan have allowed for deeper engagement and understanding of the conflict dynamics. These relationships have enabled the Gulf states to leverage their influence and provide a platform for constructive dialogue.

Saudi Arabia, for instance, has historically maintained strong ties with Sudan and has been actively involved in resolving the conflict. The Kingdom has hosted peace talks and provided financial assistance, demonstrating its commitment to supporting Sudan's stability. Similarly, the UAE has worked closely with

Sudan, focusing on youth empowerment, education, and economic development. These bilateral relationships have allowed for greater coordination between the Gulf states and Sudan, reinforcing their joint commitment to conflict resolution.

4. LESSONS LEARNT AND FUTURE PROSPECTS

The Gulf states' contributions to conflict resolution in Sudan offer valuable lessons for future endeavours. Firstly, sustained diplomatic engagement is crucial for achieving lasting peace. Conflict resolution is a long-term process that requires continuous dialogue, support, and commitment from all parties involved. The Gulf states' consistent participation and support throughout the mediation processes demonstrate the importance of ongoing engagement and perseverance.

Secondly, inclusive negotiations that involve all relevant stakeholders are essential. The complex and multifaceted nature of the conflict in Sudan necessitates the participation of diverse groups to ensure comprehensive and lasting solutions. The Gulf states have ensured the inclusion of rebel groups, civil society organisations, and marginalised communities in peace talks, recognising that sustainable peace requires addressing the needs and aspirations of all affected parties.

Lastly, the role of external actors in conflict resolution should be coordinated, consistent, and supportive of local efforts. International actors must align their strategies and resources to enhance the effectiveness and legitimacy of the peace process. The Gulf states' involvement has been characterised by coordinating with regional and international partners, ensuring a coherent approach to conflict resolution in Sudan.

To Sum Up

The extended case study of Gulf states' contributions to conflict resolution in Sudan comprehensively examines the importance of international cooperation, financial aid, diplomatic efforts, and mediation in resolving protracted and complex conflicts. The Gulf states' sustained engagement in Sudan has undeniably played a significant role in advancing the region's peace, stability, and development. By leveraging their diplomatic influence, financial resources, and bilateral relationships, the Gulf states have facilitated dialogue, provided essential aid, and strengthened the capacity of local actors to address the underlying causes of conflict.

However, achieving lasting peace in Sudan requires continued commitment, collaboration, and support from the international community, including the Gulf states. This chapter underscores the importance of addressing the underlying drivers of conflict and pursuing an inclusive, comprehensive approach to conflict resolution in Sudan and other conflict-ridden regions. The lessons learnt from the Gulf states' contributions can guide efforts towards a sustainable and peaceful future for Sudan, emphasising the need for sustained engagement, inclusive negotiations, and coordinated international support.

16

Case Study (4)

CONFLICT RESOLUTION
EFFORTS IN LIBYA AND SYRIA

Libyan and Syrian conflicts have been among the most devastating and complex in recent history. Both countries have experienced prolonged violence, political instability, and humanitarian crises. International efforts to resolve these conflicts have been challenging due to the involvement of various regional and global actors with conflicting interests. This case study examines the conflict resolution efforts in Libya and Syria, exploring the different approaches taken and the outcomes achieved.

Background

LIBYA:

The conflict in Libya began in 2011 with the popular uprising against Muammar Gaddafi's regime. NATO forces' intervention contributed to Gaddafi's overthrow, but it also created a power vacuum and led to the country's fragmentation. Since then, Libya has been plagued by armed groups, political divisions, and a struggle for control over its vast resources.

SYRIA:

The Syrian conflict originated in 2011 as a result of wide-spread protests against President Bashar al-Assad's regime. The government's violent crackdown on the demonstrations, coupled with the rise of extremist groups, transformed the conflict into a full-scale civil war. The involvement of regional and international powers further complicated the situation, leading to a protracted battle with devastating consequences for the Syrian population.

Conflict Resolution Efforts in Libya

1. UNITED NATIONS-LED INITIATIVES:

- In 2014, the UN Support Mission in Libya (UNSMIL) launched a political dialogue process to resolve the conflict peacefully. Several negotiations were held, but the process faced challenges due to ongoing fighting and the need for more consensus among critical factions. The UN also facilitated the Libyan Political Agreement in 2015, establishing the Government of National Accord (GNA) as a unified government. However, the GNA struggled to gain legitimacy and solidify its control over the country, leading to continued instability.

- Following the failure of the political dialogue process, the UN initiated the Berlin Conference in 2020. The conference aimed to unite various local, regional, and international actors to support a peaceful resolution in Libya. The meeting resulted in a comprehensive agreement encompassing a ceasefire, withdrawal of foreign forces, and demobilisation of armed groups. However, despite the initial optimism, the agreement's implementation could have been faster. Libya continues to face challenges on the path to sustainable peace.

2. REGIONAL MEDIATION:

- Efforts were made by neighbouring countries, mainly Tunisia and Algeria, to facilitate dialogue between the rival factions in Libya. These countries hosted several rounds of talks and initiated confidence-building measures. Still, they needed help to gain the trust and cooperation of the conflicting parties. The complexity of the conflict and the involvement of external actors posed challenges to achieving a sustainable resolution.

- The African Union has also been involved in mediation efforts in Libya. In 2021, the AU launched the African Union Initiative on Libya to facilitate an inclusive and Libyan-led dialogue process. The initiative emphasised the importance of preserving Libya's territorial integrity, promoting political inclusivity, and addressing the root causes of the conflict. While the initiatives by regional actors have demonstrated the commitment of neighbouring countries to finding a peaceful resolution, significant hurdles remain in reconciling the differing interests of key stakeholders.

3. EXTERNAL INTERVENTION:

- Several external powers, including Egypt, Qatar, Turkey, and the United Arab Emirates, have been involved in the Libyan conflict, supporting different factions. Their interventions often exacerbated the conflict rather than contributing to a peaceful resolution. These external actors had divergent interests and supported rival factions, prolonging the conflict and making it challenging to reach a negotiated settlement.

External actors' role in Libya also extended to providing military support to various factions. The influx of weapons and the involvement of mercenaries from multiple countries intensified the conflict, leading to further escalations and destabilisation. While some attempts have been made to enforce arms embargoes and limit the flow of foreign fighters, practical implementation has proven to be a significant challenge.

Conflict Resolution Efforts in Syria

1. GENEVA PROCESS:

- Through its Special Envoy for Syria, the United Nations launched multiple rounds of negotiations known as the Geneva process. These talks aimed to unite the Syrian government and opposition groups for a political settlement. Different rounds of negotiations were held, but they faced significant obstacles, including the unwillingness of the Assad regime to engage in meaningful negotiations and the lack of unity among opposition groups. While some progress was made, the process needed to resolve the conflict comprehensively.

Nevertheless, The Geneva Process served as an essential platform for Syrians to voice their concerns, establish trust-building measures, and identify areas of potential agreement. It also allowed the international community to engage in diplomacy and encourage dialogue between the conflicting parties. However, the lack of enforcement mechanisms and the continued violence on the ground hindered the efficacy of the process.

2. ASTANA PROCESS:

- Russia, Turkey, and Iran launched the Astana process in 2017 as an alternative track to the Geneva process. It aimed to establish de-escalation zones, monitor ceasefires, and facilitate dialogue between the Syrian government and opposition groups. Through the Astana process, several agreements were reached that contributed to reducing violence in some areas. However, it did not lead to a comprehensive political solution, as the underlying factors driving the conflict remained unaddressed.

The Astana process demonstrated regional actors' pivotal role in influencing the course of the conflict. Cooperation between Russia, Turkey, and Iran became instrumental in managing the conflict dynamics and establishing temporary ceasefires. However, the process also highlighted the challenges posed by differing strategic objectives and competing interests among these actors, ultimately limiting the negotiations' effectiveness.

3. ROLE OF INTERNATIONAL ACTORS:

- Various international actors, including the United States, Russia, Turkey, and Iran, have been involved in the Syrian conflict, supporting different factions. These competing interests have often hindered efforts to reach a peaceful resolution. The external support provided to different parties has prolonged the conflict, fuelling violence and deepening divisions within Syrian society. Similarly, these actors' international rivalry and geopolitical considerations have further complicated the situation, making it difficult to find common ground and forge a united approach towards peace.

- The involvement of external actors has also had significant implications for the humanitarian situation in Syria. The provision of military support, economic assistance, and diplomatic backing has influenced the balance of power and further deepened the suffering of the Syrian population. The delivery of humanitarian aid has often been politicised, adding to the challenges faced by relief organisations and exacerbating the humanitarian crisis.

Outcomes and Challenges

Libya and Syria continue to face significant challenges in their quest for peace and stability. The lack of a unified government, armed militias, and external interference have hindered progress towards a sustainable peace agreement in Libya. The country remains divided, with different factions vying for power and control over territories and resources. Similarly, in Syria, the ongoing violence, deep-rooted divisions, and international rivalries have impeded efforts to find a lasting solution. The devastation caused by the conflict has led to a massive humanitarian crisis, with millions of people displaced and in need of assistance.

The complexity of the conflicts in Libya and Syria has posed significant challenges to conflict resolution efforts. The involvement of various regional and international actors with divergent interests has often led to competing agendas and power struggles, making it difficult to achieve a consensus and forge a united approach towards peace. The lack of trust among the conflicting parties and their unwillingness to compromise has also hindered progress.

Additionally, the conflicts have been further complicated by extremist groups such as ISIS, which have taken advantage of the power vacuums and the chaos in both countries. These groups have posed a threat to regional and international security and have contributed to the perpetuation of violence.

Furthermore, the humanitarian crises in both Libya and Syria have been exacerbated by the conflicts. The displacement of millions of people, the destruction of infrastructure, and the limited access to necessities have created severe hardships for the civilian populations. Security concerns, bureaucratic obstacles, and political manipulation have often hindered the provision of humanitarian aid.

Despite these challenges, conflict resolution efforts have had some positive developments. The various initiatives and dialogues, whether led by the United Nations or regional actors, have provided frameworks for discussion and a platform for the conflicting parties to voice their concerns. These processes have also highlighted the importance of inclusivity, political representation, and addressing the root causes of the conflicts.

Furthermore, ceasefire agreements and de-escalation efforts, such as those established through the Berlin Conference in Libya or the Astana process in Syria, have contributed to temporary reductions in violence and improved humanitarian access in certain areas. Although limited in scope, these steps have provided some respite for the affected populations.

Sustainable peace in Libya and Syria will require a comprehensive and inclusive approach to addressing the underlying political, social, and economic grievances that have fuelled the conflicts. It will also necessitate greater cooperation among regional and international actors to find common ground and align their efforts towards a peaceful resolution. Additionally, there needs to be a commitment from all parties involved to comply with ceasefire agreements, restrict the flow of weapons, and support the delivery of humanitarian assistance.

Ultimately, resolving the conflicts in Libya and Syria will require a long-term and multi-faceted approach that addresses the disputes' symptoms and root causes. This includes promoting good governance, strengthening institutions, supporting reconciliation efforts, and ensuring the meaningful participation of all stakeholders. These conflicts can be resolved through sustained and collective actions, establishing the path to peace and stability.

17

The Role of Economic Interests in Gulf Conflict Resolution

In the complex landscape of Gulf conflict resolution, economic interests play a crucial and multifaceted role in shaping the outcome of negotiations and facilitating dialogue between warring parties. The region's economic prosperity heavily relies on stability and peace, making economic factors a significant driver of conflict resolution initiatives. This chapter delves deeper into the intricate relationship between economic interests and conflict resolution in the Gulf by exploring the various dimensions through which economic considerations influence negotiations, mediations, and the overall resolution process.

1. Economic Interdependence and Cooperation

The Gulf countries have long recognised the interdependence of their economies and the need for cooperation to foster development and stability. Economic integration is a fundamental characteristic of the Gulf Cooperation Council (GCC), which brings together countries such as Saudi Arabia, the United Arab Emirates, Qatar, Oman, Bahrain, and Kuwait. This interconnectedness has created economic incentives for conflict resolution and provided a foundation for constructive dialogue and diplomatic efforts.

The Gulf region, rich in oil and gas reserves, accounts for a significant portion of the world's energy production and distribution. This strategic advantage has led to economic interdependence among Gulf countries, with oil serving as a crucial source of revenue for their economies. As a result, protecting oil production and ensuring regional stability have become shared interests. Any disruption to oil supplies due to conflicts or tensions can have far-reaching consequences within the Gulf and globally. The reliance on oil revenue has necessitated cooperation and dialogue between Gulf countries to ensure steady production and maintain market stability, making conflict resolution imperative.

Furthermore, beyond the energy sector, the Gulf countries heavily engage in bilateral and multilateral trade, maritime trade routes, and infrastructure development projects. These economic activities have fostered cooperation and trust among

Gulf nations, creating a conducive environment for conflict resolution.

2. Wealth Redistribution and Socioeconomic Inequality

Socioeconomic disparities and grievances have occasionally fuelled conflicts in the Gulf region. Identifying and addressing these underlying economic root causes is essential in conflict resolution. Gulf countries have tried to reduce income inequality and promote social cohesion.

Governments in the Gulf have implemented various initiatives to address socioeconomic grievances to improve living conditions, create job opportunities, and reduce disparities. Wealth redistribution mechanisms, social welfare programmes, and inclusive economic growth strategies have been focal points in addressing grievances and reducing tensions. By focusing on inclusivity and providing opportunities for marginalised communities, Gulf nations aim to address the socioeconomic factors contributing to conflicts and create an environment conducive to conflict resolution.

Additionally, Gulf countries have recognised the significance of investing in education and human capital development in reducing socioeconomic disparities. By prioritising education reform and vocational training programmes, governments are equipping their populations with the necessary skills for the job market, addressing the root causes of discontent and contributing to conflict resolution efforts.

3. Economic Diplomacy and Mediation Tools

Economic diplomacy plays a significant role in conflict resolution efforts in the Gulf. Countries often leverage their financial power, trade relations, and investment incentives to encourage dialogue and promote peaceful settlements. Economic sanctions, trade agreements, and investment opportunities can influence the behaviour of warring parties and encourage them to engage in negotiations.

Gulf countries, often acting as intermediaries, utilise their economic clout to bridge the gaps and facilitate constructive dialogues between conflicting parties. The financial leverage that Gulf nations possess from their vast oil and gas reserves enables them to influence critical actors involved in regional conflicts or elsewhere. By offering economic incentives, financial aid, or investment opportunities, Gulf countries can create an atmosphere conducive to dialogue and encourage conflict resolution.

Furthermore, Gulf states have played an instrumental role in hosting international conferences and mediating regional conflicts. Economic cooperation and development have been identified through these platforms as critical components of post-conflict reconciliation. Gulf nations have successfully contributed to conflict resolution and peacebuilding by engaging in economic diplomacy and utilising mediation tools.

4. Reconstruction and Post-Conflict Development

The aftermath of conflicts in the Gulf region requires a proactive approach towards reconstruction and development. While conflict resolution aims to end violence, addressing the consequences and initiating processes that foster stability and growth is crucial. Gulf countries are committed to investing in affected regions, facilitating economic recovery, and ensuring long-term stability.

Following conflicts, Gulf states have undertaken comprehensive post-conflict reconstruction efforts, focusing on rebuilding infrastructure, restoring essential services, and revitalising the economy. Initiatives focused on employment creation, infrastructure development, and institution-building help restore trust and promote sustainable peace while mitigating the risk of a resurgence in violence.

Moreover, Gulf countries have recognised the importance of addressing the underlying causes of conflicts through long-term development strategies. By investing in social infrastructure, diversifying their economies, and promoting regional economic cooperation, Gulf nations aim to create opportunities for all citizens, reduce grievances, and secure a prosperous future.

5. *Economic Dividends of Conflict Resolution*

Successfully resolving conflicts in the Gulf leads to significant economic dividends for the countries involved. These dividends include increased investor confidence, excellent foreign direct investment, boosted regional trade, and enhanced market access. By resolving conflicts, Gulf nations create a conducive environment for economic progress, strengthening diplomatic ties and increasing collaboration and cooperation.

Gulf countries' commitment to conflict resolution positively influences investor sentiment and fosters economic stability. A peaceful and stable environment offers a platform for businesses to thrive, attracting domestic and international investment. Resolving conflicts contributes to regional integration and trade facilitation, expanding market access and increasing regional economic cooperation. These economic dividends benefit the countries directly involved and the broader Gulf region as economic prosperity becomes more attainable.

TO SUM UP

The multifaceted role of economic interests in Gulf conflict resolution is undeniable. Understanding and leveraging economic interdependence, promoting cooperation, and addressing underlying socioeconomic grievances are essential for successful negotiations and peacebuilding efforts. By recognising the significance of economic factors, stakeholders can effectively utilise economic incentives, facilitate dialogue, and deploy economic diplomacy strategies to resolve regional conflicts. The pursuit of financial stability and prosperity remains a central pillar in fostering sustainable peace in the Gulf and ensuring the well-being of its nations and people.

18

The Impact of the Ukraine War on Gulf Conflict Resolution Initiatives

The Ukraine war, which erupted in 2014 as a result of Russia's annexation of Crimea and the ongoing conflict in Eastern Ukraine, has had far-reaching consequences across the globe. Though geographically distant from the Gulf region, the competition has indirectly impacted the dynamics of conflict resolution initiatives in the Gulf, shaping the approach and priorities of Gulf countries. This chapter will delve deeper into how the Ukraine war has influenced Gulf conflict resolution efforts and the subsequent implications for regional stability.

A primary effect of the Ukraine war on Gulf conflict resolution initiatives has been a heightened focus on territorial integrity and sovereignty. Russia's annexation of Crimea highlighted the vulnerability of borders and triggered concerns among Gulf countries regarding safeguarding their territorial integrity. In a region where disputes over land and maritime boundaries are not uncommon, the Ukraine crisis served as a wake-up call, prompting Gulf countries to reevaluate their security apparatus and prioritise stability and protection of national sovereignty.

Gulf countries, particularly those near conflict zones, have recognised the urgent need to fortify their borders and prevent external threats from infiltrating their territories. Increased investments have been made in military capabilities, border patrol systems, and intelligence-sharing arrangements to respond swiftly to potential hazards. The Ukraine war has acted as a catalyst for Gulf countries to bolster their defence capabilities and emphasise the importance of maintaining territorial integrity in conflict resolution processes.

Furthermore, the Ukraine war has underscored the significance of international alliances and partnerships in resolving conflicts. The annexation of Crimea and the subsequent armed conflict in Eastern Ukraine triggered a wide range of international responses, including sanctions, diplomacy, and military support. Gulf countries observed the impact of collective action and international support on conflict resolution outcomes, leading them to place a greater emphasis on collaboration and cooperation.

Recognising the limitations of unilateral action, Gulf countries have actively engaged in coalitions and alliances to address regional conflicts. For instance, in Yemen, a team led by Saudi Arabia, with the backing of several Gulf countries, was formed in response to the ongoing conflict. This coalition aimed to restore stability, protect Yemeni sovereignty, and counter external threats. By joining forces with like-minded regional and international actors, Gulf countries have demonstrated a readiness to cooperate and coordinate efforts, recognising that collective action is essential for achieving their conflict resolution goals.

Additionally, the Ukraine war has served as a cautionary tale for Gulf countries regarding the hazards of proxy wars and foreign interventions. The involvement of various external actors in the Ukrainian conflict, including Russia and Western powers, has highlighted the risks associated with regional conflicts escalating into broader geopolitical struggles. This realisation has prompted Gulf countries to exercise caution and adopt a more measured approach in their conflict resolution strategies.

Gulf nations have become increasingly wary of being drawn into proxy wars or becoming a battleground for external powers vying for influence. They prioritise safeguarding national sovereignty and avoid entanglement in conflicts that may have unintended consequences or attract unnecessary foreign interventions. Instead, Gulf countries advocate for diplomatic solutions, valuing independent decision-making and seeking peaceful settlements through mediation, negotiation, and dialogue.

Moreover, the Ukraine war has accentuated the significance of diplomatic channels and negotiations in resolving conflicts. The inability to find a peaceful resolution to the Ukrainian crisis through diplomacy has emphasised the critical role of dialogue and negotiation processes in conflict resolution efforts. Gulf countries have recognised the need for sustained diplomatic engagement and dialogue between conflicting parties, acting as mediators and facilitators between warring factions in various regional conflicts.

By actively promoting diplomacy, Gulf countries have aimed to prevent conflicts from escalating into full-blown wars, recognising that dialogue provides a pathway to de-escalation and peaceful settlements. They engage in shuttle diplomacy, host peace talks, and support international mediation efforts to foster dialogue and promote peaceful resolutions. This emphasis on diplomatic engagement has been instrumental in shaping the Gulf's conflict resolution strategies.

Lastly, the Ukraine war has illuminated the necessity of comprehensive and sustainable peacebuilding efforts. The prolonged duration of the Ukrainian conflict and the complexities involved in resolving it have underscored the significance of addressing underlying causes, promoting reconciliation, and ensuring long-term stability. Gulf countries have taken note of these lessons and integrated comprehensive peacebuilding approaches into their conflict resolution initiatives.

Recognising that conflicts are often rooted in political, economic, and social grievances, Gulf countries have expanded their conflict resolution efforts beyond military responses. They focus on initiating political reforms, fostering inclusive governance structures, addressing socioeconomic disparities, and promoting transitional justice mechanisms. By addressing systemic issues and grievances at their root causes, Gulf countries aim to pave the way for sustainable regional peace.

In conclusion, the Ukraine war has profoundly impacted Gulf conflict resolution initiatives. It has heightened Gulf countries' focus on territorial integrity and sovereignty, underscored the significance of international alliances, emphasised the risks of proxy wars and foreign interventions, accentuated the importance of diplomatic channels and negotiations, and shed light on the necessity of comprehensive peacebuilding efforts. By considering these lessons, Gulf countries can adapt and refine their conflict resolution approaches to contribute to a more peaceful and stable Gulf region.

19

The Future of Conflict Resolution in the Gulf

As we delve into the future of conflict resolution in the Gulf, we must reflect on the progress made in this field and consider the challenges ahead. The Gulf region has been characterised by geopolitical tensions, regional rivalries, and protracted conflicts, making conflict resolution a critical endeavour for the stability and development of the area. This extended chapter will explore potential pathways for future conflict resolution efforts in the Gulf.

1. Enhanced Diplomatic Engagement

Moving forward, Gulf countries need to prioritise diplomacy as a conflict resolution. While some diplomatic efforts have been successful in the past, strengthening and enhancing these efforts is crucial. This entails fostering more sustained and open dialogue, engaging in constructive negotiations, and utilising practical diplomacy tools to bridge differences. Gulf nations should actively participate in regional and international forums to foster peace and security, further the principles of diplomacy, and build trust among each other.

Diplomatic engagement should involve finding areas of common interest and building on shared objectives. This approach can create a positive cycle of cooperation that may spill over into other conflict areas. Additionally, Gulf countries could engage in confidence-building measures, such as joint military exercises and exchanges, to reduce tensions and build trust amongst their military establishments.

2. Strengthening Track II and People-to-People Initiatives

To promote lasting peace and reconciliation, it is imperative to involve civil society organisations, experts, and citizens in conflict resolution. Track II diplomacy, which involves unofficial and non-governmental dialogues, can be pivotal in building bridges, promoting dialogue, and generating creative solutions. These informal channels provide opportunities for frank discussions away from the constraints of formal diplomatic settings.

People-to-people initiatives, including cultural exchange programmes, educational collaborations, and grassroots movements, can also contribute to reducing tensions and nurturing understanding among different communities in the Gulf. These initiatives should aim to transcend traditional divides and build connections among people on a human level, fostering empathy and a shared sense of identity beyond political and national borders.

3. Building Regional Mediation Capacities

Gulf countries should invest in building their internal mediation capacities to mediate regional conflicts effectively. This involves training diplomats to specialise in mediation and negotiation skills, including mediation courses in diplomatic training programmes, and establishing specialised mediation institutions that can facilitate peaceful resolution to disputes.

By harnessing the potential of regional mediators, Gulf countries can play a more proactive role in de-escalating tensions and resolving regional conflicts. Furthermore, establishing a network of regional mediation institutions would allow for the exchange of best practices and joint training programmes and support collaboration between countries in resolving conflicts effectively.

4. Emphasising Conflict Prevention

Preventing conflicts before they erupt is crucial for the future stability of the Gulf region. Efforts should be made to address root causes, such as socioeconomic disparities, political grievances, and identity-based tensions, through inclusive governance, economic development, and social reforms.

By focusing on conflict prevention, the Gulf can work towards creating a more peaceful and harmonious environment for its nations and communities. This entails investing in education, healthcare, infrastructure, and job creation to address the underlying causes of conflict and provide opportunities for all. Moreover, Gulf countries should emphasise the inclusion of marginalised groups, women, and youth in decision-making processes, as their meaningful participation can contribute to a more inclusive and sustainable peace.

5. Engaging in Multilateral Initiatives

Multilateral forums and organisations offer platforms for collective decision-making and conflict resolution. Gulf countries should actively engage in regional and international organisations to address common challenges, share experiences, and seek collective solutions.

Through these initiatives, Gulf nations can contribute to shaping regional security architectures that prioritise peaceful resolutions and provide a platform for exchanging best practices.

Collaborating with international partners allows for a broader range of perspectives and expertise in developing effective conflict-resolution strategies. For instance, the Gulf Cooperation Council (GCC) can continue significantly promoting dialogue, cooperation, and conflict resolution within the region.

6. Strengthening Legal Frameworks and Agreements

To ensure sustainable and enforceable conflict resolution, Gulf countries should work towards strengthening legal frameworks and agreements. This involves prioritising the signing and ratification of international treaties, conventions, and protocols that promote peace, disarmament, and the resolution of conflicts in a peaceful manner.

By adhering to international law and adopting mechanisms for dispute resolution, including arbitration and adjudication, Gulf countries can foster an environment of trust and accountability, laying the groundwork for peaceful coexistence. Establishing local and regional judicial bodies specifically focused on mediating and resolving conflicts could further augment the legal mechanisms available for conflict resolution.

TO SUM UP

The future of conflict resolution in the Gulf hinges on the willingness of regional actors to adopt a more collaborative and inclusive approach. By fostering diplomatic engagement, strengthening people-to-people initiatives, building mediation capacities, emphasising conflict prevention, engaging in multilateral initiatives, and strengthening legal frameworks and agreements, the Gulf countries can chart a course towards a more peaceful and prosperous future.

The Gulf region can only overcome its conflicts and lay the foundation for a harmonious coexistence through sustained commitment and collective effort. As conflicts evolve, the journey towards lasting peace will require adaptability, pragmatism, and a relentless pursuit of dialogue and understanding. The challenges are vast, but with a comprehensive and multifaceted approach, the Gulf region has the potential to transform conflict resolution and build a brighter future for generations to come.

Conclusion

A WAY FORWARD FOR CONFLICT RESOLUTION IN THE GULF

This chapter provides further insight into potential solutions for resolving conflicts in the Gulf region. Throughout this book, we have extensively examined historical contexts, conflict resolution techniques, and case studies to comprehensively understand the complexities and dynamics involved in resolving conflicts within and beyond the Gulf states.

The Gulf region has been marked by a complex web of conflicts and tensions, both internal and external, that have posed significant challenges to peace and stability. These conflicts are deeply rooted in historical grievances, territorial disputes, religious and sectarian divides, and struggles for power and influence. However, upon closer examination, we find that beneath the surface of intractability, there have been instances of progress and hope in conflict resolution efforts.

One of the critical factors contributing to the advancement of conflict resolution in the Gulf region is recognising the need for national reconciliation processes. Countries such as Iraq and Yemen have initiated national dialogue and reconciliation efforts to address the root causes of internal conflicts, promote inclusivity, and pave the way for post-conflict stability. Although challenging and lengthy, these processes have brought together disparate factions and provided them with a platform to voice their concerns, grievances, and aspirations. This participatory approach has played a significant role in fostering understanding, building trusted relationships, and developing a sense of collective ownership in charting a path towards sustainable peace.

An instrumental component in conflict resolution in the Gulf is the role of external powers in mediating differences between Gulf countries. The involvement of regional and international actors can bring fresh perspectives, diverse expertise, and resources to the table. Mediation efforts by countries such as Kuwait, Oman, and Qatar have demonstrated their ability to bridge divides, facilitate dialogue, and promote reconciliation among conflicting parties. These mediators leverage their diplomatic relationships, cultural understanding, and neutrality to create conducive environments for meaningful negotiations. The success of these efforts serves as a testament to the power of diplomacy and dialogue in overcoming even the most entrenched conflicts.

Moreover, transregional challenges have emerged as significant threats to the stability and security of the Gulf region. Issues such as illegal migration, drug trafficking, terrorism, and the proliferation of weapons pose substantial risks that transcend national boundaries. Combating these challenges requires a comprehensive and coordinated response from Gulf countries and the international community. By pooling their resources, sharing intelligence, and implementing joint security initiatives, the Gulf states can effectively address these threats and prevent their escalation into full-blown conflicts. It is essential to strengthen regional partnerships, enhance information-sharing mechanisms, and promote cooperation to preserve peace and security in the Gulf region.

In addition to confronting local conflicts, the Gulf countries have demonstrated their commitment to conflict resolution in broader regional contexts. Their involvement in countries such as Sudan, Libya, and Syria have showcased their willingness to contribute to peace and stability beyond their borders. Through diplomatic negotiations, humanitarian aid, and capacity-building efforts, the Gulf states have shown their dedication to resolving conflicts, supporting post-conflict reconstruction, and helping societies rebuild and thrive. These efforts benefit the recipient countries and contribute to the security and stability of the Gulf region as a whole.

Nonetheless, it is crucial to recognise the impact of external events on Gulf conflict resolution initiatives. The Ukraine war, for example, has had far-reaching consequences in terms of straining relations between Gulf countries and Russia. These tensions have permeated the regional dynamics of conflict resolution, making it challenging to find common ground and progress towards lasting peace. Moreover, the Middle East's geopolitical rivalries and proxy conflicts have further complicated the path to resolution. Creative and cooperative measures must be pursued to mitigate these challenges and foster an environment conducive to productive dialogue, trust-building, and conflict resolution.

In conclusion, conflict resolution in the Gulf necessitates a multifaceted and nuanced approach encompassing national reconciliation processes, mediation by external powers, addressing transregional challenges, active engagement in broader regional conflicts, and managing external influences. Gulf countries must sustain dialogue, promote empathy, and seek mutually beneficial compromises to resolve disputes peacefully. The commitment to conflict resolution should be coupled with efforts to address root causes, promote social justice, and strengthen good governance to prevent the recurrence of conflicts in the future.

The Gulf states can advance stability, security, and prosperity through persistent efforts, cooperation, and a steadfast commitment to lasting peace. Conflict resolution in the Gulf is an arduous task. Still, with perseverance and the strategic application of practical tools and approaches, a brighter future, characterised by harmonious coexistence, sustainable development, and enhanced regional cooperation, is within reach for the region and its people. The challenges may be formidable, but the potential for transformative change and enduring peace in the Gulf is immense.

References For Further Reading

BIBLIOGRAPHY

ʿabd Al-Hādī Khalaf, Giacomo Luciani, and Markaz Al-Khalīj Lil-Abḥāth. 2006. *Constitutional Reform and Political Participation in the Gulf.* Dubai: Gulf Research Center.

Abdel Ghafar, Adel, and Silvia Colombo. 2021. *The European Union and the Gulf Cooperation Council: Towards a New Path.* Singapore: Palgrave Macmillan.

Almezaini, Khalid S, and Jean-Marc Rickli. 2016. *The Small Gulf States.* Taylor & Francis.

Altomonte, Carlo, and Massimiliano Ferrara. 2014. *The Economic and Political Aftermath of the Arab Spring.* Edward Elgar Publishing.

Anoushiravan Ehteshami. 2013. *Dynamics of Change in the Persian Gulf: Political Economy, War and Revolution.* New York: Routledge.

Baraldi, Claudio, and Vittorio Iervese. 2013. *Participation, Facilitation, and Mediation.* Routledge.

Barany, Zoltan. 2021. *Armies of Arabia: Military Politics and Effectiveness in the Gulf.* New York, NY Oxford University Press.

Bercovitch, Jacob, and Karl R Derouen. 2011. *Unraveling Internal Conflicts in East Asia and the Pacific: Incidence, Consequences, and Resolutions.* Lanham, Md: Lexington Books.

Bercovitch, Jacob, and Scott Sigmund Gartner. 2008. *International Conflict Mediation.* Routledge.

Brynen, Rex, Bahgat Korany, and Paul Noble. 2016. *The Many Faces of National Security in the Arab World.* Springer.

Cordesman, Anthony H. 2018. *Bahrain, Oman, Qatar, and the UAE: Challenges of Security.* Boulder: Taylor and Francis.

Davidson, Christopher M. 2011. *Power and Politics in the Persian Gulf Monarchies.* New York: Columbia University Press.

Douglas Hamilton Johnson. 2003. *The Root Causes of Sudan's Civil Wars.* Indiana University Press.

Etheredge, Laura. 2011. *Persian Gulf States: Kuwait, Qatar, Bahrain, Oman, and the United Arab Emirates.* New York: Britannica Educational Pub., In Association With Rosen Educational Services.

Federica Bicchi, Benoit Challand, and Steven Heydermann. 2018. *The Struggle for Influence in the Middle East.* Routledge.

Fraihat Ibrahim Fraihat. 2020. *Iran and Saudi Arabia.* Edinburgh University Press.

Fredline M'cormack-Hale, and Commonwealth Secretariat. 2012. *Gender, Peace and Security: Women's Advocacy and Conflict Resolution.* London: Commonwealth Secretariat.

Furuya, Shuichi, Hitomi Takemura, and Kuniko Ozaki. 2023. *Global Impact of the Ukraine Conflict.* Springer Nature.

Gaub, Florence, Strategic Studies Institute, and S Army. 2015. *The Gulf Moment.* Lulu.com.

Greenberg, Melanie C, John H Barton, and Margaret E Mcguinness. 2000. *Words over War: Mediation and Arbitration to Prevent Deadly Conflict.* Lanham, Md: Rowman And Littlefield Publ.

Guerette, Rob T. 2016. *Migration, Culture Conflict, Crime and Terrorism.* Routledge.

Guidero, Amanda, and Maia Carter Hallward. 2018. *Global Responses to Conflict and Crisis in Syria and Yemen.* Springer.

Henner Fürtig. 2002. *Iran's Rivalry with Saudi Arabia between the Gulf Wars.* Ithaca Press (GB).

Hichem Karoui. 2012. *Arab Spring.* Createspace Independent Publishing Platform.

Houghton, Benjamin, and Kasia A Houghton. 2023. *China, Russia, and the USA in the Middle East.* Taylor & Francis.

Hourly History. 2021. *The Gulf War.* Independently Published.

Hunter, Dale. 2012. *The Art of Facilitation.* Penguin Random House New Zealand Limited.

Ibrahim Zabad. 2019. *Middle Eastern Minorities: The Impact of the Arab Spring.* New York, NY: Routledge.

Jawad, Saad N. 2022. *Iraq after the Invasion.* Palgrave Macmillan.

Jones, Jeremy. 2012. *Oman, Culture and Diplomacy.* Edinburgh University Press.

Khalid Al-Jaber, and Dania Thafer. 2019. *The Dilemma of Security and Defense in the Gulf Region.* ISD LLC.

Kienle, Eberhard, and Nadine Sika. 2015. *The Arab Uprisings.* Bloomsbury Publishing.

Kostiner, Joseph, and Springerlink (Online Service. 2009. *Conflict and Co-operation in the Gulf Region.* Wiesbaden: Vs Verlag Für Sozialwissenschaften.

Kristian Coates Ulrichsen. 2023. *Centers of Power in the Arab Gulf States.* Hurst Publishers.

Kupchan, Charles. 2012. *The Persian Gulf and the West (RLE Iran D).* Taylor & Francis.

Lackner, Helen. 2019. *Yemen in Crisis.* Verso Books.

Lin, Jing, Edward J Brantmeier, and Christa Bruhn. 2008. *Transforming Education for Peace.* IAP.

Little, David, and Tanenbaum Center For Interreligious Understanding. 2007. *Peacemakers in Action: Profiles of Religion in Conflict Resolution.* Cambridge; New York: Cambridge University Press.

Mabon, Simon. 2015. *Saudi Arabia and Iran.* Bloomsbury Publishing.

———. 2023. *The Struggle for Supremacy in the Middle East.* Cambridge University Press.

Majid Khadduri, and Edmund Ghareeb. 2001. *War in the Gulf, 1990-91: The Iraq-Kuwait Conflict and Its Implications.* Oxford: Oxford University Press.

Martini, Jeffrey, Becca Wasser, Dalia Dassa Kaye, Daniel Egel, and Cordaye Ogletree. 2016. *The Outlook for Arab Gulf Cooperation.* Rand Corporation.

Mason, Robert, and Simon Mabon. 2022. *The Gulf States and the Horn of Africa: Interests, Influences and Instability.* Manchester: Manchester University Press.

Mattar, Khawla, and May Seikaly. 2014. *The Silent Revolution.* ISD LLC.

Matthews, Ken. 2003. *The Gulf Conflict and International Relations.* Routledge.

Md Mizanur Rahman, and Amr Al-Azm. 2023. *Social Change in the Gulf Region.* Springer Nature.

Mehran Kamrava. 2011. *The International Politics of the Persian Gulf.* Syracuse, New York Syracuse University Press.

Nahla Yassine-Hamdan, and Frederic S Pearson. 2014. *Arab Approaches to Conflict Resolution.* Routledge.

Nakhleh, Emile. 1986. *The Gulf Cooperation Council.* Praeger.

Niblock, Tim. 2015. *Social and Economic Development in the Arab Gulf (RLE Economy of Middle East).* Routledge.

Niblock, Tim, Talmiz Ahmad, and Degang Sun. 2018. *The Gulf States, Asia and the Indian Ocean: Ensuring the Security of the Sea Lanes.* Berlin, Germany: Gerlach Press.

Niblock, Tim, Talmiz Ahmad, Degang Sun, and Gerlach Press. 2018. *Conflict Resolution and Creation of a Security Community in the Gulf Region.* Berlin Gerlach Press.

O Jeff Harris, and Sandra J Hartman. 2002. *Organizational Behavior.* New York: Best Business Books.

Okubo, Shiro, and Louise Shelley. 2011. *Human Security, Transnational Crime and Human Trafficking.* Routledge.

Osborne, Christine. 2022. *Old Gulf Coast Days: Sultanate of Oman*. Old Gulf Coast Days.

P.J. Vatikiotis. 2016. *Conflict in the Middle East*. Routledge.

Pavel Pylypcuk. 2017. *The Emergence and Consequences of the Syrian Civil War*. GRIN Verlag.

Rabasa, Angel, and Et Al. 2004. *The Muslim World after 9/11*. Santa Monica, Ca: Rand.

Ramazani, Rouhollah K, and Joseph A Kechichian. 1988. *The Gulf Cooperation Council: Record and Analysis*. Charlottesville: University Press Of Virginia.

Rosemarie Said Zahlan. n.d. *The Making of the Modern Gulf States: Kuwait, Bahrain, Qatar, the United Arab Emirates and Oman*. Routledge.

Rother, Mr.Bjoern, Ms.Gaelle Pierre, Davide Lombardo, Risto Herrala, Ms.Priscilla Toffano, Mr.Erik Roos, Mr.Allan G Auclair, and Ms.Karina Manasseh. 2016. *The Economic Impact of Conflicts and the Refugee Crisis in the Middle East and North Africa*. International Monetary Fund.

Rottenburg, Richard, Sandra Calkins, and Jörg Gertel. 2014. *Disrupting Territories: Land, Commodification and Conflict in Sudan*. Suffolk: James Currey.

Saddam Abdulkarim Obaid. 2023. *Yemen's Road to War*. Austin Macauley Publishers.

Salem, Paul. 1997. *Conflict Resolution in the Arab World*. Syracuse University Press.

Salomon, Gavriel, and Baruch Nevo. 2005. *Peace Education*. Psychology Press.

Sattar, Aornob. 2012. *Women's Role in Conflict Resolution*. LAP Lambert Academic Publishing.

Shakir, Farah. 2017. *The Iraqi Federation*. Taylor & Francis.

Shay, Shaul. 2019. *The Red Sea Region between War and Reconciliation*. Liverpool University Press.

Sim, Li-Chen, and Jonathan Fulton. 2022. *Asian Perceptions of Gulf Security*. Taylor & Francis.

Sune Haugbolle, and Anders Hastrup. 2013. *The Politics of Violence, Truth and Reconciliation in the Arab Middle East.* Routledge.

Terrill, Andrew. 2019. *The Saudi-Iranian Rivalry and the Future of Middle East Security.* Strategic Studies Institute.

Ulrichsen,Christian Coates. 2014. *Qatar and the Arab Spring.* Oxford Oxford University Press.

Ulrichsen, Kristian. 2016. *Gulf States in International Political Economy.* Houndmills, Basingstoke, Hampshire: Palgrave Macmillan.

Unesco. 2011. *The Hidden Crisis: Armed Conflict and Education.* Paris United Nations Educational, Scientific And Cultural Organization.

Wai, Dunstan M. 1981. *The African-Arab Conflict in the Sudan.* Africana Pub.

Wallensteen, Peter. 2006. *Understanding Conflict Resolution: War, Peace and the Global System.* Sage Publications Ltd.

Wilkenfeld, Jonathan, Kathleen Young, David Quinn, and Victor Asal. 2007. *Mediating International Crises.* Routledge.

Zhuying Zhou, Jonathan Spangler, and SpringerLink (Online Service. 2018. *Cultural and Educational Exchanges between Rival Societies: Cooperation and Competition in an Interdependent World.* Singapore: Springer Singapore.